To Nana Enjoy!

Food, Fun & Fabulous

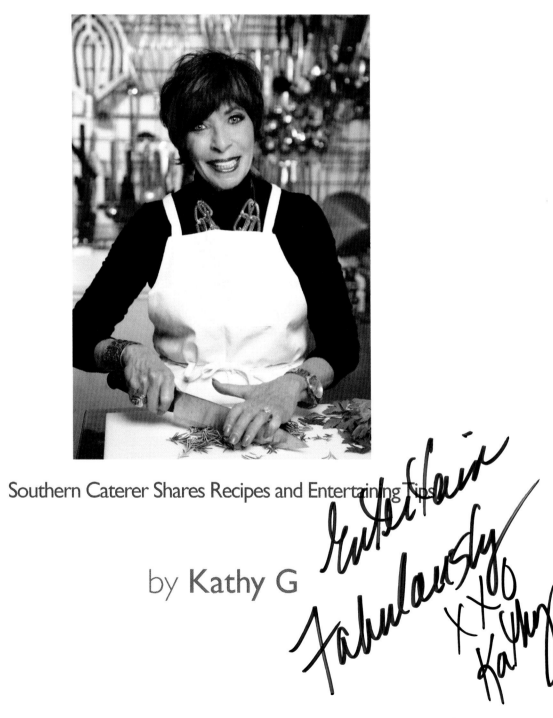

Southern Caterer Shares Recipes and Entertaining Tips

by Kathy G

Entertain Fabulously
xxoo
Kathy G

Published by

inspired
intermedia

Inspired Intermedia
5815 Richwater Drive
Dallas, Texas 75252
972-898-8915
www.inspiredintermedia.com

Publisher: Brian G. Carabet
Author: Kathy G. Mezrano
Managing Editor: Rosalie Wilson

For information about custom editions, premium and corporate books, please contact brian@inspiredintermedia.com

Printed in USA

PUBLISHER'S DATA

Food, Fun and Fabulous

Library of Congress Control Number:
2015957646

ISBN 13: 978-09969653-3-0

First Printing 2015

10 9 8 7 6 5 4 3 2 1

dedication

To my parents for their love of good food and for always being open to sharing it at table with others.

To my husband for his unconditional love and support in all my endeavors.

Food, Fun & Fabulous

Southern Caterer Shares Recipes and Entertaining Tips

"Kathy Mezrano incorporates her cosmopolitan style of entertaining and cooking into this beautiful new cookbook where she shares her flavorful, bright and delicious recipes that have made her the most outstanding caterer in Alabama. Her multi-cultural approach to cooking selects the most exciting flavors from around the world and combines them together in a way that would make Martha Stewart proud. Her tips on entertaining are full of clever, practical ideas that will propel any home cook into a dazzling designer of special celebrations. Kathy is one of those rare individuals who creates recipes that anyone can produce--each packed with personality and all arranged with a keen eye for beauty that go together to make a party an unforgettable occasion."

*- **Frank Stitt,***
James Beard Award Winner,
Restauranteur and Author

Restaurants:
Highlands Bar and Grill,
Bottega, Chez Fon Fon

contents

Turkey pitas with raspberry honey mustard

introduction

"When I'm entertaining, I see the whole vision. It's not just about the food, the flowers, music or decor — it's about the complete experience."
- Kathy G

Good food is meant to be shared and recipes are too, which is why I've created this collection of all-time favorites. Some are family recipes that have been around for generations, others are twists on popular dishes, and still more are new flavors developed by my son Jason, who's also our company's executive chef. All of them have proven themselves time and again as frequently requested Kathy G. & Company dishes. Beyond the recipes, you'll find lots of ideas for styling and presentation, because I believe that a dinner party should engage all the senses in a creative way. I love being a hostess and I have been one all my life, even with my kids. From setting the table to having all the "colors" or food groups represented, I've always felt that one element was as important as the other for the total experience.

Having been immersed in the world of fine food since a child and an active part of the growing

catering scene for several decades, I know first-hand that fabulous food makes a party great, and thoughtful presentation makes it memorable. This book is not intended as an exhaustive, step-by-step listing of how to host a party and exactly what to serve. Rather, it's meant as a creative springboard, offering imaginative themes and a variety of ways to tailor the offerings and presentation to your unique needs and preferences. You'll find a full range of recipes, from fast and simple treats you can have on hand in case someone drops by to elaborate appetizers, entrées, sides, drinks, and desserts that make a statement on formal occasions. The photography shows grand-scale events because that's the level where I dream, though any of the themes or recipes work just as well for an intimate meal at home.

My ideas on food, family, and how a good meal or party brings everyone together in a special way—they're more than philosophies, they're our family legacy. I'm proud of my Lebanese heritage as well as my Southern roots and what it means in the realm of hospitality. Growing up, my parents made the dining room the center of our lives. They loved good food and made everyday meals feel special through their creativity, thoughtful presentation, and attention to detail. Anyone was welcome to drop by for a home-cooked meal, anytime. To this day, my friends fondly remember my parents' generosity and the good food they prepared. Sunday dinners were especially important to our family because my father made a point to always be home—he worked very hard in a demanding career as a wholesale produce buyer.

Dad insisted on tasting everything he bought in order to ensure quality for his restaurateur clientele. For many years, he serviced major accounts in greater Birmingham, including landmarks like The Bright Star Restaurant that trusted him to provide the absolute best. Naturally, my father allowed his work to carry over into his private life in all the best ways. We always had an abundance of beautiful, fresh produce at home and an appreciation for how great meals begin with fine-quality ingredients. He and my mother

were warm and extremely giving, and they planned and catered several church suppers once a month—my sister and I were always invited to be part of the project, whether setting the tables or preparing the meals.

I'm by no means a chef, but I know my way around the kitchen, I appreciate good food, and I have been blessed with so many opportunities to produce grand affairs, from event planning, décor, and floral design to full-scale catering. I suppose you could say my career started in college, when I'd throw elaborate parties for friends—some people stayed up late partying, others were studying, but I was getting décor ready for my next get-together and enjoying every moment. Interestingly, my formal entrée to the event world came after a casual acquaintance—who had attended a themed surprise birthday party I'd orchestrated—suggested that I start catering professionally. I never had a business plan, I just started giving parties and people loved them and the referrals kept coming.

I'm a firm believer in joining industry associations and have learned from networking with my peers across the country. Serving on the board of The International Caterers Association gave me a wealth of experience that I've shared over the years throughout our company. We've been blessed to have won industry awards at the national level.

I've had the support of family since the beginning— my mother helped cook and my mother-in-law did a lot of the prep work. Kathy G. & Co. grew like crazy, and my husband eventually left his law practice to help oversee the business side of things. I am forever grateful for his unconditional love and support. And our son, Jason, who thankfully redirected his studies from public relations to the culinary world so long ago, has served as the executive chef for more than a decade now.

Jason and Kathy

Today, we're not only considered Birmingham's premier caterer, we also offer event design and floral design. And we have a fabulous venue, The Gardens Café by Kathy G. at the Birmingham Botanical Gardens, that plays host to dozens of weddings and special events each year. Over the past years, we have been an exclusive caterer to The Birmingham Museum of Art, The Alys Stephens Performing Arts Center, and Park Lane of Mountain Brook as well as The Historic Donnelly House and Zoo Lodge. We cater parties of two and parties of thousands— they're all different and they're all deliciously beautiful. Whether you're treating yourself to a gourmet meal or sharing one with family or friends, I hope you find joy in the journey and make memories galore. ✳

"Every tabletop is a stage waiting for the curtain to go up!"
- Kathy G

Start with a White Plate

It's absolutely amazing how much you can accomplish with a simple white plate. Think about what you want the event to feel like and then just layer in the accessories that speak to you. Casual summertime brunch? A bright placemat, a fun napkin folded to showcase the pattern, and colorful flatware and stemware. This has a totally different vibe than the sleek black and white setting. And displaying a beautiful napkin with a coordinating ring and using two-tone flatware sets a completely different tone. An entirely different statement is made with the formal setting with an ornate and coordinating salad plate—notice what the presence and placement of the flatware says about the many delicious courses to come. So, start with what you have and get creative with the rest!

hors d'oeuvres

Hors d'oeuvres are a first impression, and you only get one of those. And everybody's heard the old saying that you taste first with your eyes—well, it's true. Whether you're making everything from scratch or adding in a few gourmet premade items, present the appetizers beautifully and you'll wow your guests. When your guests fall in love with the appetizers, they'll decide that dinner tastes great too, even before they take their first bite. The small portion nature of hors d'oeuvres means that they are a great way to introduce guests to really bold flavors. Couple those bold flavors with tried-and-true favorites, and you have yourself the makings of a very successful party.

Truffled Mushroom Crostini

yield: 10 - 12 pieces

The mushroom mixture is so divine. You can use it as a condiment with grilled or braised meats. It makes a lovely hors d'oeurve paired with goat cheese on a crisp crostini. It will keep for 2-3 days in the fridge and is easy to assemble and have ready before guests arrive.

Crostini

1 French baguette

Boursin cheese

chives, chopped (for garnish)

Slice baguette into ¼-inch slices and arrange on a baking sheet. Bake at 350 degrees for 5-7 minutes or until crispy but not too dry. Remove from oven, set aside, and allow to cool.

Mushroom Mixture

2-3 cups sliced mushrooms (choose 2-3 varieties)

2 tablespoons butter

1 tablespoon rosemary, chopped

1 tablespoon thyme, chopped

1 tablespoon parsley, chopped

2 cloves fresh garlic, minced

2 tablespoons olive oil

2 tablespoons truffle oil (plus extra for finishing)

salt and pepper to taste

1 goat cheese log or Boursin whipped

Heat olive oil and butter in a sauté pan on medium-high heat. Add mushrooms and garlic, stirring occasionally with a wooden spoon. Cook mushrooms until tender and lightly browned, about 3-4 minutes. Add herbs and truffle oil, season with salt and pepper.

Spread 1 ½ teaspoons goat cheese onto crostini. Top with 1 tablespoon mushroom mixture. Garnish with fresh chopped chives and finish with truffle oil. Crostinis and mushroom mix can be made 2 days ahead. Assemble just before serving. Serve warm or at room temperature. Garnish with shaved parmesan.

Caramelized Onion and Gruyere Tartlets

yield: 12 tartlets

These are really mini quiches. You can pour the mixture into a pie shell for a lunch item. They freeze beautifully and can be reheated to serve.

2 teaspoons butter

1 tablespoon vegetable oil

1 small Vidalia onion, finely diced

pinch of salt

3 eggs, whisked smooth

1 ½ cups half-and-half

salt and pepper to taste

3 pie dough sheets or 12 (2-ounce) pre-cooked tart shells

1 cup gruyere cheese, grated

Preheat oven to 350. Heat butter and vegetable oil over low heat. Add onions and pinch of salt. Cook until tender and slightly browned. Whisk eggs and half-and-half until smooth. Season with salt and pepper. Spray mini muffin pans with non-stick pan spray. Roll pie dough sheets to ¼ inch. Cut rounds out of the pie dough—you want it half an inch wider than the mini muffin tins. Line the sprayed tins with cut-out rounds of dough. Pierce small holes in bottoms of pie dough. Par-bake dough for 5-8 minutes. Let cool. Place 1 teaspoon of caramelized onions and 1 ½ teaspoons gruyere cheese in each muffin tin. Top with egg mixture until just below the top of dough. Bake for about 8-10 minutes, or until eggs are completely set. Let cool for a few minutes and carefully remove tartlets from tin with fork. Serve warm.

Crudités in Mini Pilsner with Dips

yield: 12 - 15 pilsners

I love this presentation for individual portions of crudities and dips. Everyone likes to double dip but nobody likes to share other people's double dipped appetizers, so this is an appealing option. I like to arrange larger amounts by cutting all the vegetables vertically and standing them up in glass cubes.

Crudites

3 carrots, peeled

2 zucchini, quartered lengthwise

2 yellow squash, quartered lengthwise

3 celery stalks, quartered lengthwise

Cut each vegetable into sticks about 3 inches long and ¼-inch wide. Keep chilled until you are ready to assemble. You can use any vegetable you prefer.

Green Goddess Dip

yield: 3 cups

2 cups parsley (1 large bunch), trimmed and packed

1 cup fresh basil leaves

4 tablespoons fresh chives, chopped

1-2 tablespoons fresh tarragon, chopped (or 1-2 teaspoons dried)

6-8 scallions, chopped

1 lemon, zested and juiced

1 cup mayonnaise

½ cup sour cream

2 garlic cloves, peeled

2 teaspoons Dijon mustard

salt and pepper to taste

In food processor, combine first 5 ingredients and blend for 5 seconds. Add the remaining 6 ingredients and blend until smooth, scraping sides down occasionally. Season with salt and pepper. Cover and chill.

Red Pepper Cream Dip

yield: 2 cups

12 ounces cream cheese (room temperature)

½ cup roasted red peppers, drained (jar or freshly made)

1 tablespoon lemon juice

¼ cup half-and-half

In a food processor with a blade, blend all ingredients until smooth.

To assemble, fill mini pilsner glasses with dip of choice ⅓ full. Stick a few crudité in each pilsner. Serve cold.

Spinach Herb Dip

yield: 4 cups

1 (10-ounce) package frozen spinach, defrosted and squeezed

½ cup parsley, chopped

½ cup green onions, chopped

½ teaspoon dill weed

1 cup mayonnaise

1 cup sour cream

½ teaspoon oregano

½ teaspoon lemon juice

Combine all ingredients.

Belgian Endive Leaves

yield: 24 pieces

I can't say enough about using Belgian endive "petals" as an hors d'oeuvre vehicle. Just separate them and use them to scoop dips or fill them with cheeses, chicken salad, crab salad, or even tabouli. They have a great visual impact and add a nice crisp crunch to any dish.

5 heads white Belgian endive leaves

5 cups crumbled blue cheese

2 cups cream cheese

3 cups walnuts or 1 cup fresh raspberries

¼ cup fresh parsley, chopped

Cut the leaves at the base and fan out on a sheet pan. Place on top of lemon-soaked paper towels to retain color. In a mixer, whip cream cheese until soft. Add blue cheese. Mix for 3-5 minutes. Place cheese in a piping bag. Toast walnuts for 5 minutes at 350 degrees. On a platter, spread out leaves, pipe cheese mixture on the end of each leaf, and top each leaf with a toasted walnut. Garnish the platter with parsley.

Grilled Peach Honey-infused Mascarpone on a Crostini

yield: 24 pieces

1 French baguette, sliced into ¼-inch slices

1 (8-ounce) container mascarpone

3 tablespoons honey

3-4 fresh peaches, cut into ½-inch-thick wedges

¼ cup fresh basil, finely shredded

Preheat oven to 350 degrees. Also preheat a hot grill or grill pan. Brush sliced bread with olive oil and place on a baking sheet. Toast bread in preheated oven for 5-7 minutes, making sure to not burn the bread or allow the bread to have any color. In food processor, whip mascarpone and honey until smooth. Grill peach wedges on hot grill or grill pan, allowing nice grill marks on both sides. On cooled crostini, spread small amount of honey mascarpone mixture, add grilled peach, and garnish with basil. Optional: wrap peach in thinly sliced proscutto.

Mini BLTs with Remoulade

yield: 8 pieces

Everyone loves a BLT so this hors d'oeuvre is always a winner. It's a cinch to serve if you have all the ingredients ready to assemble just before guests arrive.

Mini BLTs

8 slices white or wheat sandwich bread

3-4 thick slices of apple-smoked bacon

4 teaspoons light brown sugar

4 ripe Roma tomatoes

4 teaspoons extra virgin olive oil

8 arugula leaves

2 cups remoulade sauce

Using a biscuit cutter, cut the bread into either rounds or squares and toast in the oven at 325 degrees for 5-8 minutes until bread is light brown. Lay apple-smoked bacon on a sheet pan. Lightly cover bacon with brown sugar and bake until crispy. Cut bacon into same-size pieces as the rounds. Slice tomatoes ¾-inch thick. Lay out the rounds on a platter. Place arugula on top of bread. Add 1 teaspoon of remoulade sauce on top of arugula. Place tomato slice on arugula. Top with slice of warm candied bacon with a dot of remoulade sauce to finish.

Remoulade

yield: 4 cups

3 cups mayonnaise

1 cup Creole/spicy mustard

¼ cup fresh lemon juice

⅓ cup chopped parsley

½ cup chopped capers

4 tablespoons green onions

4 tablespoons sweet pickle relish

½ cup whole grain mustard

salt and pepper to taste

Mix all ingredients together and season to taste.

Savory Cheesecake Varieties

These cheesecakes make a lovely display. They're easy to assemble and freeze beautifully, just be sure to defrost them before adding final toppings. The crust recipe can be used for all savory cheesecakes.

Crust

yield: 1 cake

2 packs of butter crackers like Ritz

1 stick butter, melted

Crumble crackers in processor. Add butter. Spray spring form pan with pan spray and press cracker mixture to form crust.

Blue Cheese Cheesecake

6 (8-ounce) blocks cream cheese

1 pound blue cheese

pinch of cayenne

2 eggs

2 pears, diced small

2 tablespoons butter

¼ cup brown sugar

3 peeled pears, small diced

3 tablespoons butter

3 tablespoons brown sugar

Mix cream cheese, blue cheese, cayenne, and eggs in mixer. Pour mixture over crust in spring form pan. Cook in water bath at 325 degrees for 40 minutes. If cake is getting too brown on top and still not done, cover and continue baking for 10-15 minutes, or until done. Over medium heat, melt butter, then add diced pears and sauté for 3 minutes. Add brown sugar and stir well. Cook pears for about 5 minutes. Let cool. Garnish cheesecake with caramelized pears.

Another option is to garnish with cranberry chutney in place of pears.

Fiesta Cheesecake

6 (8-ounce) blocks cream cheese

pinch of salt

pinch of ground cumin

pinch of chili powder

½ can diced green chilies

2 eggs

Mix all ingredients in mixer. Pour mixture over crust in spring form pan. Cook in water bath at 325 degrees for 40 minutes. Cover cake for another 10-15 minutes., if not done.

Topping for Fiesta Cheesecake

1 cup sour cream

¼ cup green onions, sliced

½ cup Rotel tomatoes, drained

½ cup black olives, sliced

2 cups cheddar, shredded

When cake is cooled, spread sour cream over the entire top of cheesecake. Top with cheddar cheese, covering the sour cream. Cover with Rotel, tomatoes leaving 1 inch around the boarder so cheese is visible. Top with black olives, 1 inch less than Rotel. Place green onions in center of cake.

Mango Cheddar Cheese Cheesecake

6 (8-ounce) blocks cream cheese

4 cups cheddar cheese, shredded

¾ jar mango chutney

2 eggs

½ cup curry powder

2 cups crushed pecans

Combine cream cheese, cheddar cheese, chutney, eggs, and curry powder in mixer. Pour mixture over crust in spring form pan. Top with a layer of mango chutney and crushed pecans. Cook in water bath at 325 degrees for 40 minutes. Cover cake for another 20 minutes. After cake is cooled, remove from pan and add crushed pecans around the edge.

Goat Cheese Logs with Toppings

yield: 1 log

Always keep a goat cheese log on hand. In summertime, just chop fresh tomatoes and fresh basil and then top with a drizzle of extra virgin olive oil and freshly cracked pepper. Serve with water crackers or sliced crostini.

Goat Cheese Logs

8 ounces goat cheese (chevre)

4 ounces cream cheese

In mixer with paddle attachment, combine goat and cream cheeses and beat until well blended, 3-4 minutes. Place cheese mixture on plastic wrap and roll tightly into a log approximately 2 inches in diameter and 6 inches in length. Serve with tomato and oil topping or rolled in dried cranberry and nut topping.

Tomato and Olive Oil Topping

¼ cup dry sundried tomatoes

5-6 whole garlic cloves, peeled

1-2 sprigs fresh rosemary (plus 2-3 sprigs for garnish)

1 cup olive oil (or blended oil)

Pesto Mixture (page 46)

In small sauce pan on medium heat, cook garlic cloves in oil. Be careful not to burn garlic. Cook garlic until golden brown, 15-20 minutes. Take pan off stove and allow to cool completely. In an air-tight container, pour olive oil with garlic over tomatoes and rosemary. Store in refrigerator. After a couple of days, remove rosemary as it will become brown. The flavor will be infused within the oil. To serve: spoon a small amount of tomatoes and garlic over goat cheese log and serve with choice of crackers. Garnish with fresh rosemary sprigs.

Dried Cranberry & Nut Topping

1 cup dried cranberries, rough chopped

½ cup toasted nuts, chopped (walnuts, pecans)

Preheat oven to 350 degrees and place nuts on baking sheet. Toast nuts for 8-10 minutes, being careful not to burn them. Remove nuts, set aside, and let cool completely. Finely chop cranberries and cooled nuts and mix together.

Place cranberry and nut mixture onto a work surface or shallow dish wide enough to roll the goat cheese log around. Press log into mixture, roll, and cover all sides. Place on serving platter and serve with crackers of your choice. Garnish with whole nuts and cranberries.

Prosciutto-wrapped Honeydew Melon

yield: 24 servings

I've turned an Italian classic into a fun visual hors d'oeuvre. I like to place it on the end of a fork, standing up, in a wheat grass flat. It can be wrapped and placed on a pick as well.

1 small melon (honeydew or cantaloupe)

¼ pound prosciutto, very thinly sliced

24 mint leaves, small

Carefully remove outer rind from melon. Cut melon in half and remove seeds. Use melon baller to make balls. Place mint around melon balls, wrap with prosciutto to cover completely, and secure with toothpicks or skewers. Serve chilled and right away.

Create Tablescapes for Memorable Parties

Tablescape is our go-to word for beautiful presentations of all sorts of food. Food can't just taste good, it needs to be beautifully presented too. You could spend thousands of dollars on gorgeous serveware and dinnerware—and goodness knows it's fun—but really you just need the basics and a few great accessories to create a beautiful tablescape. This tablescape functions as both a lush centerpiece and bountiful spread. To complete this mouth-watering arrangement, add cut vegetable dippers, assorted cheeses and crackers, and other finger foods to the colorful vegetable foundation.

Building a base:

A coffee table provides a convenient location for the appetizer buffet. To build the foundation for the vegetables, begin by positioning large serving pieces. To protect the table surface, select a piece for the front that will cover a large area. Or, if desired, cover the table with plastic wrap. Later you can tuck the excess edges of the wrap underneath the vegetables. Choose a variety of bowls, baskets, and platters to lend textural interest. Use a large breadboard or cutting

board in the front to hold the cheeses, spreads, and crackers. Stack serving pieces at the back of the table to add height to the arrangement for visual appeal.

Adding the Lush Fillers:

Fill out the arrangement with some large, uncut vegetables that will not be eaten. Group the vegetables together by color, ensuring that color is evenly spaced around the table. Leftover vegetables need not be wasted; use for soups sautés, or salads. Place whole vegetables in and around the baskets to build up the foundation. To make it easy for guests to serve themselves, leave space for plates and napkins. Hollow out at least one large head of cabbage to fill with dip. Fill in empty spaces with kale or seasonal greenery. Flowers may be added as well.✳

Serveware Essentials

I've created a short list of ingredients and accessories to have on hand for quick, spur-of-the-moment hors d'oeuvres so that you're ready for unexpected company. In addition to this list, you'll want some basic serving platters to make entertaining easy and give the presentation a wow effect—after all, presentation is just as important as taste. Here are the essentials: white rectangular platters in varying sizes, 12-inch oval platters, a wooden bowl for salads, a couple of small white bowls for saues and dips, and a lovely basket for chips and crackers. I would start out with a basic white collection and then branch out into other looks such as copper and pottery for rustic appeal.

Items to Have On Hand

Basic Ingredients

applewood-smoked bacon

baguettes

Belgian endive

black and green olives

carrots and celery

crackers

flatbreads

fresh herbs

goat cheese logs

pastry shells

phyllo shells

prosciutto

Home-mades or Ready-mades

chicken salad

guacamole

hummus

pesto

pimento cheese

salsa

Accessories

Asian boxes and chopsticks

bamboo picks and skewers

craft paper for cones

mini acrylic pilsners or shot glasses

rock salt

wheat grass flats

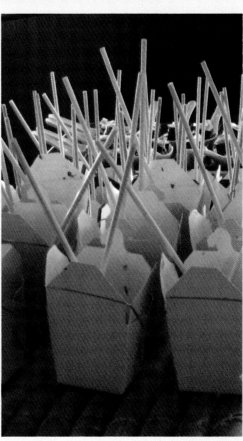

southern buffet

Southern food traditions are helping to re-shape the culinary landscape across the country. The South has an abundance of wonderful produce, meat, and seafood, with plenty of opportunities to recreate the past. The soul food of the South ranges by region, from the Low Country of Charleston to the Mississippi Delta. The Gulf Coast provides renowned seafood including red snapper, royal red shrimp, and Apalachicola Bay oysters. Many signature dishes come from recipes that are passed down from generation to generation, so you have the immediate emotional connection of home. Watching my mother make homemade cornbread in a cast-iron skillet with hot bacon grease—or the potlicker from my dad's collard greens and ham hocks—is a fond memory of my youth. The black-eyed peas we had for New Year's Day and the BBQ pork family dinner are Southern traditions that date back to the colonial days. My spin on these timeless recipes keeps the flavors we love and presents them in a fresh way that works great for an upscale meal or a buffet. The Mac & Cheese muffins are an updated way to make my mother's traditional macaroni and cheese, the crab cakes use local Gulf Coast crab, and the fried green tomatoes are a famous Southern dish—all are special recipes from the family.

Shrimp and Grits

yield: 4

Shrimp and Grits is a traditional dish in the Low Country of coastal Alabama as well as the Carolinas. It's traditionally served as a breakfast dish, but it makes a wonderful station at parties and receptions. It's probably our most requested food station for events.

Base

2 ½ tablespoons olive oil

½ cup yellow onion, diced

¼ cup celery, diced

¼ cup red bell peppers, diced

¾ cup bacon, finely chopped

1 teaspoon garlic, minced

Dry Mix

1 teaspoon parsley

¼ teaspoon thyme

¼ teaspoon oregano

½ teaspoon basil

¼ teaspoon cayenne

¼ teaspoon garlic powder

¼ teaspoon onion powder

1 medium bay leaf

Sauce

1 tablespoon white wine

3 cups canned chopped tomatoes

3 cups sea clam juice

1 teaspoon lemon juice

1 tablespoon hot sauce

salt and pepper to taste

1 pound large shrimp, peeled, de-veined, tail off

Roux

4 tablespoons butter, melted

4 tablespoons flour

Garnish

¼ cup parsley, chopped

¼ cup scallions, thinly sliced

In medium-sized pot, make base. Heat oil. Sauté bacon until golden brown. Add onions, celery, bell peppers, and garlic and cook for 10-15 minutes. Add spice mix to base mixture and cook for 5 minutes, stirring occasionally. Deglaze mixture with the white wine. Puree canned tomatoes in processor. Add tomatoes and clam juice to stockpot and cook for 20-25 minutes, until mix comes to a boil, stirring often. Add lemon juice and hot sauce to sauce mixture, season with salt and pepper, and continue to cook for 5 minutes. In a separate skillet make roux by melting butter and whisking in the flour. Take off heat. Add shrimp and continue cooking until shrimp are fully cooked, about 10-12 minutes. Keep stirring. Slowly add roux to tomato mixture until thick. Add salt and pepper to taste. Garnish each serving with parsley and scallions.

Grits

yield: 8 servings

Grits of course is a Southern staple. Add grated sharp cheddar for breakfast cheese grits or any cheese of choice for a side dish.

2 cups stone-ground grits

6 cups water

I stick butter

2 cups heavy cream

I ½ cups parmesan, grated

salt and pepper to taste

Bring water and butter to a boil in a pot. Pour in grits slowly while whisking. Continue to stir constantly and cook grits until soft and creamy. Stir in the heavy cream and parmesan cheese. Season with salt and pepper. Cook 20-25 minutes. Add more liquid if needed.

Crab Cakes with Lemon Aioli

yield: 12 mini or 4 large

Who doesn't love these delicious cakes? We serve them on a lime slice topped with lemon aioli or as a luncheon side with confetti slaw.

1 pound jumbo lump crabmeat, picked

2 eggs, beaten

1 tablespoon shallots, minced

2 teaspoons chives, minced

1 ½ tablespoons lemon juice

1 teaspoon Old Bay seasoning

2 tablespoons olive oil

2 tablespoons unsalted butter, melted

salt and fresh-ground black pepper to taste

2 ½ cups panko

2 beaten eggs in small bowl for egg wash

Combine crab, shallots, chives, and seasoning in a large bowl. Gently stir in eggs and butter, then add ½ cup of the panko. Divide mixture into 12 portions. Dip each cake into egg wash, then roll in the remaining bread crumbs. Form into 2-inch round cakes. In a hot sauté pan, sear in oil and butter until golden brown. Finish in 350-degree oven.

Lemon Aioli

yield: 2 cups

2 egg yolks

1 teaspoon creamy Dijon mustard

2 tablespoons lemon juice

½ teaspoon kosher salt

pinch of black pepper

1 teaspoon sugar

1 ¼ cups olive oil

2 tablespoons parsley, chopped

In a mixing bowl set on top of a damp dish cloth (to prevent slipping), whisk egg yolks, mustard, lemon juice, salt, pepper, and sugar together until thick and creamy, about 1 minute. Add the oil in a thin, steady stream, whisking constantly until thick and glossy. Be careful not to add the oil too fast. Stir in the parsley. May be done in a food processor: place ingredients in bowl then slowly drizzle oil through the feed tube.

Juniper-marinated Quail with Port Wine Glaze

yield: 8 servings

We use the Bob White semi-boneless quail and cut each bird in four sections for easy pickup hors d'oeurves. Quail hunting is an old tradition in the South and hunters would bring home enough to feed several families a delicious supper, which would be served up with hot biscuits, rice, and sorghum syrup.

4 semi-boneless quail

2 tablespoons toasted, finely ground juniper berries

2 tablespoons olive oil

1 teaspoon kosher salt

1 teaspoon fine-ground black peppercorns

2 sprigs fresh rosemary

1 teaspoon fresh garlic, chopped

Combine all ingredients in a mixing bowl and toss until the quail are well seasoned; wrap and refrigerate overnight. Remove rosemary sprigs. On a medium-hot grill, grill quail until medium or medium-well, about 5-7 minutes, turning to prevent burning. Do not overcook. Quarter the quail and drizzle with port wine glaze.

Port Wine Glaze

1 ½ cups port wine

½ cup red wine

1 tablespoon granulated sugar

Combine all ingredients in small, heavy-bottom saucepan. Over medium-high heat, reduce mixture until only 1 cup of liquid remains and it is the consistency of syrup.

Stuffed Mushrooms with Sausage and Pecans

yield: 24 pieces

These are always well received at parties. You can make the mixture ahead and assemble the day of serving. Creamed spinach is an alternative filling.

24 large mushrooms

1 pound pork sausage

½ cup onion, chopped

2 tablespoons parsley, minced

1/8 teaspoon salt

½ teaspoon pepper

1 (8-ounce) package cream cheese, softened

1 cup toasted pecans, chopped

Wipe mushrooms with soft cloth. Remove mushroom stems; chop stems and set caps aside. Combine chopped stems and sausage in a large skillet; cook over medium heat, stirring to crumble, until meat is browned. Drain meat mixture into a colander and pat dry with a paper towel. Return mixture to skillet; add onions, parsley, salt, and pepper. Cook over low heat until mixture is thoroughly heated. Cool meat mixture. In a mixer fitted with the paddle attachment, beat the cream cheese until soft and smooth. Add meat mixture and pecans. Continue beating until mixed well. Place mushroom caps on an ungreased baking sheet; season with salt and pepper and bake at 350 degrees for 10 minutes. Drain juice from mushrooms and cool. Spoon sausage mixture into mushroom caps. Bake at 350 degrees for 5-10 minutes.

Fried Green Tomatoes

yield: 6-8 pieces

Try a different spin on your BLT with a slice of fried green tomatoes. We serve them with a spicy remoulade sauce at events. You can use the same technique for okra.

3 large green tomatoes

1 cup milk

2 eggs

1 cup all-purpose flour

3 cups cornmeal

½ teaspoon garlic powder

½ teaspoon onion powder

½ teaspoon cayenne pepper

½ teaspoon fresh ground black pepper

2 tablespoons kosher salt

6 cups vegetable oil

Heat oil in cast iron skillet to 350 degrees. Slice large green tomatoes into $\frac{1}{3}$-inch-thick slices. Combine eggs with milk and set aside. Combine ½ cup flour, cornmeal, garlic powder, cayenne pepper, salt, and pepper in a shallow pan. Place remaining ½ cup flour in a shallow pan. Cooking instructions: dredge tomato slices in flour, dip tomato slices in the egg mixture, dredge tomato slices in cornmeal mixture, fry the breaded tomato slices for 3-5 minutes on each side until golden brown, drain on paper towels or a rack, and sprinkle hot tomatoes with salt.

Mac & Cheese Muffins

yield: 2 dozen

This comfort food makes a wonderful hors d'oeurve. Easy to eat and perfect for all ages.

1 pound elbow macaroni

3 cups whole milk

¼ cup butter

¼ cup flour

1 cup parmesan, grated

3 cups cheddar, shredded

2 eggs

salt and pepper to taste

Cook macaroni according to package. In medium pot, heat milk over medium heat. In small sauce pan, melt butter then whisk in flour to make a paste. Add the paste and parmesan to the hot milk and continue to cook, whisking constantly, until mixture simmers and becomes thick and smooth. Pour cheese sauce over the cooked macaroni and add 2 cups of the cheddar cheese. Season with salt and pepper and stir well. Spoon mixture into a well-buttered mini muffin pan and top with remaining cheddar cheese. Bake at 350 degrees for 12-15 minutes, until cheese is melted and cooked through.

Pimento Cheese

yield: 3 cups

This is definitely a Southern tradition. My mother always made this spread for her bridge group. We add more mayo to use it as a dip.

1 pound sharp yellow cheese

3 large red bell peppers, roasted, peeled, seeded, and chopped

½ cup homemade mayonnaise or best-quality commercial mayonnaise

splash of Tabasco or Siracha

Finely shred the cheese by hand or in a food processor with the grating wheel. Transfer the grated cheese to a mixer, add the peppers, mayonnaise, Tabasco, and blend all together thoroughly. Refrigerate and serve chilled. The spread will keep for several days in the refrigerator.

Pecan-crusted Oysters

yield: 12 pieces

Delicious and divine served individually on a silver spoon, passed or plattered.

½ cup pecan pieces

¼ cup all-purpose flour

1 ½ cup plain cornmeal

1 teaspoon smoked paprika

pinch of cayenne (optional)

¼ teaspoon garlic powder

¼ teaspoon onion powder

½ teaspoon white pepper

1 teaspoon salt

½ teaspoon fresh thyme, chopped

1 dozen oysters, pre-shucked and cleaned in liquid (medium size) or 1 can

1 quart canola oil (or peanut oil)

To make breading, pulse pecans in food processor about three times until rough-chopped (not a powder). Add flour, cornmeal, and spices, and mix together to create a dry mix and place in a bowl. Gently roll each oyster (shucked, cleaned, and drained) in breading. Pour oil in medium-size pot and heat to 400 degrees. Use a hot oil thermometer to check temperature or use a home fryer system. Place breaded oyster into heated oil. Deep fry oyster on each side for 1-2 minutes, or until the crust turns golden brown. Overcrowding oysters in the pan will make it difficult to fry them properly without affecting the integrity of the breading. Remove from pan with slotted spoon, drain on paper towel and serve immediately.

Bacon-wrapped Chicken

yield: 8 servings

Of course, everything's better with bacon! I like the applewood-smoked bacon for the flavor plus it keeps the chicken breast moist. This recipe will also work well with boneless thighs.

8 boneless chicken breasts

12-16 slices applewood-smoked bacon

salt and pepper to taste

Trim any fat off the chicken breast and season with the salt and pepper. Lay out a slice of bacon and wrap around the chicken breast. You may have to use more than one slice of bacon to wrap the breast. Use toothpicks to keep the bacon in place. Place the wrapped chicken on a sheet pan with space between them. Preheat oven to 400 degrees. Cook the chicken for 7 minutes then turn the oven down to 350 degrees and cook an additional 10-15 minutes or until the bacon is done and the internal temperature of the chicken reaches 160 degrees.

Mini Pecan Tarts

yield: 12

My mother was known for her pastries and she made the best pecan pies and tarts. She always used Karo syrup but molasses is a good substitute.

1 stick butter

4 ounces cream cheese

½ cups all-purpose flour

Have butter and cream cheese at room temperature. In mixing bowl with paddle attachment, mix until combined. Add flour and mix until a soft dough forms. Spray mini muffin tins and place a small dough ball in each form, approximately 1 tablespoon. Flour the handle of a wooden spoon and use it to press dough into forms and make mini pie shells.

½ cup dark brown sugar

1 stick unsalted butter, melted

½ teaspoon salt

3 eggs

½ teaspoon vanilla

2 teaspoons molasses

1 cup pecan pieces

In mixing bowl, stir together sugar, salt, and melted butter. Slowly whisk in each egg. Whisk in vanilla and molasses. Fill tart shells ¾ full of pecan pieces. Pour filling all the way to top. Bake at 325 degrees for 15-20 minutes, or until puffed and golden.

Candied Pecans

yield: 4 cups

Pecans are a staple in the Southern pantry. I like to put a spin on these and candy them for a wonderful snack. They also make a great topping for salads and desserts.

4 cups pecan halves

2 cups sugar

6 egg whites

Preheat oven to 350 degrees. In a mixer with a wisk attachment, add egg whites and sugar. Mix on medium for about 2 minutes. Pour egg mixture over pecans and stir. Place on sprayed pan. Cook for 15-20 minutes, stirring every 5 minutes. Be sure not to over-brown the pecans. Let cool.

Mint Julep
yield: 2 drinks

A traditional Southern drink made famous by the Kentucky Derby, this is always served in a silver julep cup. For a different take, try a good rye whiskey in place of bourbon. We created a mint julep bar with whiskey choices and fruit syrups.

1 cup sugar

1 cup water

40 mint leaves, plus mint sprigs (for garnish)

powdered sugar (for garnish)

2 ounces bourbon per drink

plenty of crushed ice

Combine sugar and water in small saucepan and heat to make a simple syrup. Bring to slight boil then add mint leaves. Remove from heat, let cool. Pour mixture through a fine mesh strainer to remove mint leaves. For one drink:, add 4 ounces mint syrup and 2 ounces bourbon into julep cup. Fill with crushed ice and stir. Garnish with mint sprig and top with sprinkle of powdered sugar.

Serve it Southern Style

To serve all of this fabulous food in the traditional style, you'll want to use classic silver for its elegance. If you're offering a buffet service, consider a mixture of family china—old and new, any style—for an interesting look that's still in touch with the theme. White-ware can certainly be used instead of silver or china and it's another lovely presentation option. Whatever the plates, silverware, and linen napkins are a must.

Decorate with tons of hydrangea and garden roses to give your party more of a formal, elegant look. We like to add a touch of whimsy with Chilton County peaches on silver candelabras. Citrus bases work great on the platters. The bases are easy to make using eight-inch Styrofoam rounds, green is preferred. Stack four rounds on top of each other and pin together with U-shaped florist pins. Then take four-inch floral picks or wooden skewers and insert in one end of the fruit. Use a tack hammer to nail the fruit securely on the base. Continue securing the fruit completely around the base. Then add lemon leaf or salal to fill in the gaps so the Styrofoam doesn't show.

tuscan table

You get a really great flavor fusion when you combine the best of Mediterranean, Greek, Italian, Lebanese, and other types of fare from the region. It's food that everybody loves and the dishes are great for nibbling and grazing. Our tablescape concept works really well here. Think lavish buffet, a giant antipasto station, a mezze or nosh table. It's like being at a market and getting to sample everything in sight. Simple things like hummus dips, cheeses, olives, raw and grilled veggies, breads, crackers, and cured meats can be paired with prepared dishes like crostinis, mini muffulettas, pita sandwiches, chicken skewers, mini meatballs, and whatever else sounds tasty. Most of this can be made ahead of time, which is super convenient, and you can just fill the table up, plan on a few quick replenishes, and it'll last all night. It's a great way to keep a large crowd happy—we've done it for 500—and of course small crowds love it, too. This is healthy food, so you feel good when you're enjoying it. You can easily go 100-percent vegetarian or add in some meats as desired.

Basil Cheese Terrine with Sundried Tomatoes

yield: I bundt pan or I loaf pan

I love the classic combination of flavors, and the color scheme makes it especially festive to serve during the holidays! The pesto layer holds its vibrant color with the combination of spinach and basil. The terrine may be made ahead and will keep for up to one week.

White Mixture

16 ounces cream cheese, softened

8 ounces goat cheese, crumbled (can substitute blue cheese

In food processor, process until smooth and set aside.

Green Mixture (Basil Pesto)

2 cups spinach leaves

4 cups basil leaves

4 cloves garlic

½ cup olive oil

2 cups fresh parmesan, grated

In food processor, process spinach, basil, and garlic, and with processor running, slowly add oil. Pulse in parmesan and set aside. Mixture should be thick.

Red Mixture

½ cup sundried tomatoes

4 cloves garlic, crushed

½ cup olive oil

2 cups fresh parmesan, grated

Soak sundried tomatoes for about 20 minutes and drain. In food processor, pulse sundried tomatoes with garlic, oil, and parmesan.

Line a 2-quart bundt pan with plastic wrap, allowing edges to overhang. Put white, green, and red mixtures into separate dipping bags. Spread mixtures one at a time into bundt pan, making festive holiday layers: white, green, white, red, and white. Once layers are finished, wrap tight with plastic wrap and chill the mold for 24 hours. When ready to serve, carefully open plastic wrap to access the terrine. Quickly turn mold on top of serving platter, remove remaining plastic wrap. Garnish with additional sundried tomatoes and serve with your favorite crackers or flatbread.

Marinated Olives

yield: 4 cups

I like to keep these on hand in the fridge at all times. They can be used in salads or pasta dishes and they stand alone as a delicious snack.

2 cups green queen olives, pitted

2 cups Kalamata olives, pitted

2 cloves garlic, chopped

½ cup extra virgin olive oil

½ lemon, zest plus juice

1 tablespoon rosemary, chopped

1 tablespoon thyme, chopped

2 sprigs of rosemary

pinch red pepper flakes

¼ cup parsley, chopped

Rinse and drain olives, mix well. In sauté pan, combine garlic, oil, lemon zest, and red pepper flakes and cook on low heat for 10 minutes. Remove from heat and let cool to 160 degrees. Strain oil. Pour oil over olives and add herbs. Mix well and store in cooler. Best if prepared at least 1 week prior to serving.

Chicken Kabobs

yield: 15 skewers

A perfect addition when you need a more substantial appetizer. The kabobs can be made ahead on 6-inch bamboo skewers and popped in the oven just before guests arrive.

5 boneless/skinless chicken breasts, cut into 30 two-inch cubes

¼ cup olive oil

1 tablespoon thyme, chopped

1 tablespoon parsley, chopped

1 tablespoon rosemary, chopped

2 red bell peppers, stemmed, seeded and cut into 15 two-inch cubes

½ medium onion, cut into 15 two-inch cubes

15 skewers

Mix olive oil, thyme, parsley, and rosemary. Marinate cubed chicken in olive oil and herb mixture overnight. On each skewer, alternate chicken, red pepper, chicken, and onion. Grill mark chicken and finish in oven for 10-15 minutes.

Mediterranean Crostini

The toppings will keep for 2 weeks in the fridge, so definitely make them ahead of time.

Crostini: French baguette, sliced on bias and toasted lightly in 350-degree oven.

Herbed Goat Cheese Spread
yield: 2 cups

16 ounces cream cheese

8 ounces goat cheese

pinch of salt

2 tablespoons parsley, chopped

1 tablespoon thyme, chopped

In mixer with paddle attachment, mix goat cheese and cream cheese until smooth. Add herbs and salt.

Fig Topping
yield: 2 cups

2 cups dried figs

1 cup water

1 cup red wine

Using kitchen scissors, cut stems off of figs. In a saucepan, combine figs, water, and wine. Bring to a boil and boil until figs are soft. Drain off liquid and reserve liquid. Cool figs and liquid. In food processor, puree figs adding a little of the liquid to achieve a smooth and spreadable consistency. On a crostini, cover half of the crostini with the cheese spread and the other half with the fig spread.

Tapenade Topping
yield: 3 cups

3 cups Kalamata olives, pitted, sliced in half

2 cups green olives, pitted, sliced in half

4 tablespoons parsley, chopped

4 tablespoons rosemary, chopped

1 tablespoon garlic, finely minced

1 tablespoon red wine vinegar

1 teaspoon anchovy paste

½ cup extra virgin olive oil

dash of black pepper

In a food processor combine all ingredients except olive oil. Pulse the food processor until rough-chopped (do not puree). Slowly add olive oil. Serve on toasted crostini.

Roasted Red Pepper Topping
yield: 2 cups

1 cup golden raisins

½ cup water

½ cup white wine

1 (7-ounce) can roasted red peppers, julienned

1 tablespoon parsley

1 tablespoon rosemary

1 tablespoon thyme

Combine raisins, water, and wine in a saucepot and bring to a boil. Reduce heat and simmer until the raisins plump. Drain liquid and reserve the liquid. Cool mixture and liquid. Add peppers and herbs to the raisins. Add a little of the liquid back to the mixture. Served on toasted crostini.

Trio of Hummus Dips

Hummus is wonderfully versatile. You can substitute any type of bean to achieve a different flavor. The lemon salt gives the hummus a real punch, so it's definitely worth the effort to locate some at a Middle Eastern grocery store. All of these healthy dips will keep for 1 week in the fridge. Serve with fresh pita, pita chips, vegetables, and anything else that sounds good to you.

Black Bean Dip
yield: 3 cups

1 (14-ounce) can black beans

1 garlic clove

1 tablespoon tahini

¼ cup olive oil

2 tablespoons white balsamic vinegar

½ teaspoon ground cumin

salt to taste

Rinse black beans in colander. In food processor, beat garlic with a pinch of salt to form a paste. Add the tahini and vinegar. Continue to blend and start adding black beans. Blend to consistency of peanut butter and gradually add olive oil until desired consistency. Season with cumin and salt to taste.

Roasted Red Pepper Dip
yield: 3 cups

1 (14-ounce) can chickpeas

1 clove garlic

2 teaspoons lemon juice

¼ cup olive oil

2 tablespoons tahini

1 roasted red pepper

dash lemon salt to taste

Drain chickpeas. Put garlic in a processor and puree. Add chickpeas, lemon juice, salt, tahini, and peppers. Add olive oil slowly as the full amount may not be needed. Puree until smooth consistency (if too thick, add water). Adjust seasonings.

Traditional Hummus Dip
yield: 3 cups

1 (14-ounce) can chickpeas

1 clove garlic

2 tablespoons lemon juice

¼ cup olive oil

salt to taste

dash lemon salt to taste

Drain chickpeas. In food processor, puree garlic. Add chickpeas and gradually add olive oil until smooth. Add salt and blend again. If too thick add water.

Penne Pasta Salad with Tomatoes, Feta, and Fresh Mint

yield: 4 cups

One of my favorites. The mint added at the last minute gives it such a fresh flavor. The salad can easily be made ahead, just be sure to bring it to room temperature before serving.

½ pound penne pasta

½ cup olive oil

6 cloves garlic

2 cups diced tomatoes or halved cherry tomatoes

⅓ cup goat cheese, crumbled (feta may be substituted)

3 tablespoons fresh mint, finely chopped

salt and pepper to taste

Bring large stockpot of salted water to a rapid boil and cook pasta according to package directions. Drain and set aside. Meanwhile, in a large skillet over medium-high heat, heat olive oil and garlic until garlic starts to cook, but not fry. When cloves start to brown, take oil off of heat and let the garlic flavor infuse for 5-10 minutes. Remove cloves. Pour oil over pasta a little at a time and mix noodles. The pasta needs to be wet but not soaking. The pasta will absorb the garlic-infused oil. Once pasta is cooled, add remaining ingredients and mix. Adjust seasonings as desired.

Summary Couscous Salad

yield: 12 cups

A delicious salad that works great as a main dish or a side. My son Jason developed this recipe. He likes to use the larger size Israeli couscous, though it also works with the smaller size grain.

8 cups chicken or vegetable stock

³/₄ cup olive oil

1 large red onion, cut into rounds, grilled, and chopped

2 cloves garlic, roasted in oven, and minced

½ cup carrots, peeled, cut in half lengthwise, grilled, and medium diced

½ cup zucchini, cut in half lengthwise, grilled, and medium diced

½ cup yellow squash, cut in half, grilled, and medium diced

½ cup red bell pepper, cut in half, deseeded, grilled, and medium diced

2 tablespoons parsley, chopped

3 cups Israeli couscous

½ cup golden raisins

½ cup dried cherries

¼ teaspoon ground cinnamon

¼ teaspoon ground cumin

¼ cup fresh basil, sliced

fresh ground pepper to taste

salt to taste

In small pot, heat stock with 1 tablespoon olive oil. In large bowl, add all grilled vegetables, parsley, and 1 tablespoon olive oil. Cook couscous according to package directions using stock as the liquid. When couscous is cooked, drain and add to veggies. Add remaining ingredients. Toss and serve.

Fattoush Salad

yield: 6 cups

Such a healthy salad! Make it with any combination of seasonal vegetables—heirloom tomatoes are an especially tasty addition. Have bread toasted and toss it in just before serving. There are many variations of a bread salad with vegetables—panzanella with baguette croutons or Southern style with toasted cornbread croutons.

8 tomatoes, diced

2 cups cucumbers, seeded and diced

1 large zucchini, barely grilled and diced

2 red bell peppers, seeded, grilled, and diced

$\frac{1}{2}$ cup green onions, chopped

$\frac{1}{2}$ cup Kalamata olives, sliced in half

$\frac{1}{2}$ cup basil, chopped

$\frac{1}{2}$ cup cilantro, chopped

$\frac{1}{2}$ cup parsley, chopped

6 tablespoons olive oil

$\frac{1}{2}$ cup lemon juice

2 tablespoons cumin

1 cup feta, crumbled

3 loaves Pita bread, grilled or toasted and broken into large pieces

Combine all ingredients (except feta and pita) in large bowl. Gently toss in the toasted pita. Just before serving, sprinkle feta over the top.

Orzo Salad with Lemon and Parsley

yield: 4 cups

A very clean, simple salad. For a heartier entrée, double the recipe and add shrimp or chicken.

$\frac{1}{2}$ pound cooked orzo pasta

2 tablespoons olive oil

2 cloves garlic, peeled and sliced

1 lemon, zest and juice

3 tablespoons Italian leaf parsley, finely chopped

$\frac{1}{4}$ cup pine nuts

salt and pepper to taste

In small Dutch oven or heavy stockpot, heat olive oil over low-medium heat. Sauté garlic until translucent for 2-3 minutes, being careful not to burn. Gently fold in cooked orzo pasta, lemon zest and juice, parsley, and salt and pepper. Add pine nuts, transfer to a serving bowl, and serve at room tempature.

Kibbee

yield: 13x9 pan

Kibbee is to Middle Eastern cooking what a meatball is to Italian cooking. It's a very hearty meat dish made with cracked wheat and onion. Kibbeh may be baked as a casserole or fried in smaller meatballs for an hors d'oeurve.

1 tablespoon olive oil

1 medium onion, small diced

2 tablespoons pine nuts

1 cup #1 bulgur wheat, rinsed

1 medium onion, pureed in processor

2 pounds round steak, fat and gristle removed, ground three times

ice water in a small bowl

2 teaspoons salt

1 teaspoon black pepper

½ teaspoon cinnamon

½ teaspoon cumin

4 tablespoons butter

Sauté chopped onion and pine nuts in olive oil until cooked but not browned and set aside. Rinse the bulgur wheat with cold water three times, then pour water off and leave in small bowl to soften for 10 minutes. Mix pureed onion with drained wheat, then add ground meat. Use ice water to mix by hand, adding as necessary to keep mixture cool. Add salt, pepper, cinnamon, and cumin. Mix thoroughly.

Butter a 13x9 pan, press half of the meat mixture in a thin layer, wetting hands with ice water. Sprinkle the sautéed onion and pine nut mixture over the meat. Cut small chunks of butter over the meat mixture. Add one more layer of meat and press firmly using ice water. Pull edges away from the side with a knife. Cut lengthwise into 9 slices, then cut diagonally, creating triangles. The pan should contain about 60 pieces. Bake at 400 degrees for 45 minutes.

Tabouli

yield: 3 cups

I can eat this wonderful salad every day. I remember hand-chopping the parley when I was 12 years old, long before food processors were around. My grandmother always told me I made the best when it came to tabouli. Definitely an all-time favorite of mine. It will keep for 2 days in the fridge..

½ cup #1 bulgur wheat

½ cup lemon juice

4 bunches of curly parsley, washed, stemmed, and finely chopped

4-5 tomatoes, diced

½ cup fresh mint, chopped

2 bunches of green onions, sliced or 1 medium sweet onion, diced

⅓ cup olive oil

2 teaspoons salt

1 teaspoon pepper

1 head romaine lettuce, finely sliced (optional)

In small bowl, wash wheat in cool tap water. Leave for 15 minutes, then drain and squeeze moisture out. Place wheat in bottom of salad bowl and add lemon juice. In food processor, chop parsley on pulse setting, then add to bowl. Combine all other ingredients. Toss well and serve.

Create a Tuscan Table

Tuscan tables are a great way to try out a multilevel presentation. You can set up a tablescape on a kitchen island, sideboard, or coffee table, whatever works. Just go through all of your cabinets and pull out anything that looks useful or interesting. Create different levels on the table by turning bowls upside-down and setting platters on top—just hide the mechanics of the levels with greenery or fresh produce. I like to use antique olive jars, crock bowls, wooden pizza boards, copper pieces, marble, and stone for an authentic Tuscan presentation. I always like to include pieces from Alabama-based Earthborn Pottery in our displays; my dear friend Tena Payne is the owner, and she has such an amazing line of custom-crafted pottery in a color palette that looks great with any décor. Use stacks of kale, cabbage, grapes, and whole veggies to create a bountiful presentation full of color and texture. French baguettes look great in an urn. Always fill over-sized dishes with crackers or bread broken into large pieces and let them artistically spill onto the table.

One of my event coordinators, Natalie, says when setting up a Tuscan display, "messy is good!"

greek taverna night

Oh, I had such a wonderful trip to Greece with my dear friend and her big fat Greek family—they're such warm-hearted people. The meals were divine. We looked forward to dining at a different taverna each evening and just couldn't wait to go. The small local restaurants are decorated with little twinkling lights and serve family-style meals where platters and platters of delicious food are brought out in waves. And the ouzo, I loved the ouzo. It's a drink distilled from grapes and flavored with the flowering plant anise, and it has a distinct flavor—you definitely need to develop a taste for it. It's considered an aperitif to stimulate the appetite and should be served chilled or over ice. I enjoyed the experience of dining at tavernas so much that shortly after I returned home, I hosted a taverna party for six. I've since done it for more than 60, and the concept is always so well received. It's a great type of party because the food is delicious and the camaraderie is fabulous. A lively ambience with Greek music and flowing ouzo usually leads to dancing. The following recipes are a sampling of some of the items you can serve at your next Taverna night.

Keftedes: Greek Meatballs
yield: 85 cocktail-size or 60 home-size

I usually double the recipe and freeze the extras. Just pull out the frozen meatballs and dredge and fry them as needed.

2 ½ pounds lean ground beef (or beef and lamb)

2 large onions, finely chopped

5 tablespoons olive oil

3 eggs

5 tablespoons fresh Italian parsley, chopped

5 tablespoons fresh mint, chopped

2 ½ teaspoons dried oregano

1 ½ teaspoons salt

¼ teaspoon pepper

10 slices firm (2-day-old) white bread

all-purpose flour for dredging

In a large bowl, thoroughly combine meat, onion, olive oil, eggs, parsley, mint, oregano, salt, and pepper. Moisten bread with water, squeeze, tear in pieces, and add to bowl. Mix well. Shape into ½-inch cocktail meatballs or larger home-style meatballs. When ready to cook, roll in flour and pan fry in vegetable oil.

Tzatziki Sauce
yield: 2 cups

A wonderful yogurt dipping sauce for keftedes and other Greek dishes. This will keep for up to 3 weeks in the fridge. I like to use whole-milk yogurt.

16 ounces Fage Greek yogurt

1 cucumber, peeled, seeded, and grated

3 tablespoons lemon juice

1 tablespoon fresh dill, chopped

½ teaspoon cumin

2 cloves garlic, minced

salt and pepper to taste

Peel and grate cucumber with box grater then place into a bowl. Add yogurt and remaining ingredients. Mix together with spatula, then season with salt and pepper.

Grilled Lamb Chops

yield: 8 servings

These "popsicle" lamb chops are absolutely delicious and easy to eat with a knife and fork or you can just pick them up and enjoy! Even though the fat will burn off when seared, I still like to trim the fat before cooking.

½ **cup olive oil**

4 garlic cloves, chopped

2 tablespoons dried oregano

salt and pepper to taste

2 Frenched racks of lamb (8 ribs each) with fat edge trimmed

Mix olive oil, garlic, oregano, salt, and pepper and rub on Frenched racks of lamb. Let marinate in the refrigerator for 20 minutes. Heat grill to 350-400 degrees. Place racks meat-side down for 5 minutes, then flip over and continue. Check internal temperature to medium rare (130 degrees).

Once meat reaches medium rare, let rest for 10 minutes before cutting. If cooking inside, sear whole racks in skillet until brown on both sides, then finish in 350-degree oven for 10 minutes. Check internal temperature (130 degrees). Serve with Mint Pesto.

Mint Pesto

½ **cup fresh mint, finely chopped**

½ **cup fresh spinach, finely chopped**

2 cloves garlic, finely chopped

½ **cup extra virgin olive oil**

In mixing bowl (do not use processor or mint will turn black), mix all ingredients.

Pastichio: Greek Lasagna

yield: 12-15 servings

This is made in three separate steps and then combined. It can be made 2-3 days ahead or can be frozen for 2 months.

Meat Mixture

2 pounds ground chuck

1 large onion, chopped

salt and pepper

1 (28-ounce) can crushed tomatoes

4 ounces tomato paste

2 dashes cinnamon

½ cup grated parmesan

pinch of sugar (optional)

Pasta Mixture

12 ounces ziti or pastichio

½ stick butter, melted

1 cup kefalotiri cheese, grated (can substitute romano cheese)

salt and pepper

2 whole eggs, beaten

2 egg whites, beaten

6 tablespoons butter

Cheese Sauce Mixture

½ cup flour, sifted

3 cups milk

1 cup heavy cream

2 egg yolks, beaten

²/₃ cup parmesan, grated

salt and white pepper

Brown meat over medium heat, and add onions, salt, pepper, tomatoes, paste, and cinnamon. Cook one hour. Drain most all fat from sauce. Add cheese and sugar.

Boil noodles in salted water for 7-9 minutes. Drain and rinse. Add melted butter. Add grated cheese, salt, and pepper, whole eggs, and egg whites that have been well beaten.

In small sauce pan, heat milk and cream. In medium saucepan, melt butter, then add flour and cook over medium heat, stirring constantly. Slowly add lukewarm milk mixture whisking constantly. Incorporate egg yolks with 2 tablespoons of sauce in small separate bowl then add to saucepan. Cook slowly until mixture thickens. Add parmesan, salt, and white pepper.

Pastichio assembly: Preheat oven to 350 degrees. Grease 11x15x2 pan with butter and sprinkle with bread crumbs. Spread a thick layer of macaroni in pan. Next spread meat evenly over macaroni. Spread remaining macaroni over meat layer. Pour cream sauce over all. Bake for 1 hour until golden on top. Let stand at least 20 minutes before cutting into squares.

Summary Salad

yield: 6-8 servings

This is referred to as Summer Salad since the ingredients are at their peak in the summer. It's my all-time favorite salad. In other months, you may add lettuce to the same ingredients and use roasted red peppers rather than fresh peppers.

4 large ripe tomatoes, cut in wedges

2 cucumbers, peeled, seeded, and sliced

1 green pepper, seeded, ribbed, and thinly sliced

½ red onion, thinly sliced

½ cup pitted Kalamata olives

½ teaspoon dried oregano

½ cup extra-virgin olive oil

4 tablespoons red wine vinegar

½ teaspoon sea salt

¼ teaspoon cracked pepper

1 cup crumbled feta

In medium bowl, mix tomatoes, cucumbers, bell pepper, onion, olives, oregano, olive oil, vinegar, salt, and pepper. Adjust salt and pepper to taste. Top with feta. May be made 2 hours ahead. Serve at room temperature.

Spanakopita: Spinach Pie

yield: serves 12

This may be served warm or cold. You can also freeze the pie and bake it later.

1/3 cup olive oil

1 sweet white onion, finely chopped (or 10 green onions, green and white parts)

2 pounds fresh spinach, clean and almost dry

2 tablespoons fresh parsley, finely chopped

2 tablespoons fresh dill, finely chopped

salt and pepper to taste

2 eggs, lightly beaten

8 ounces feta

4 ounces kefalograviera, grated (or Swiss)

2/3 cup olive oil

4 tablespoons melted butter

1 pound phyllo dough

Preheat oven to 350 degrees. In large skillet, heat olive oil and sauté onions until translucent. Add spinach, parsley, and dill and sauté for 3 minutes until wilted and tender. Season with salt and pepper. Remove from heat, drain any liquid, let cool slightly, add eggs and cheeses, and then stir until well combined.

Be sure to cover phyllo with dish-cloth while working to keep it from drying out. Use pastry brush to coat 13x9 baking pan with olive oil. Lay a sheet of phyllo dough in pan, fold in edges, and brush with olive oil and butter. Continue to layer 4 more sheets of phyllo, brushing each with oil and butter. Spread spinach mixture over the phyllo, then layer 5 more sheets of phyllo, brushing each with olive oil including the top sheet. With sharp knife, score Spanakopita into serving squares before baking. Bake for 40-45 minutes at 350 degrees until crisp and golden. Let rest for 5 minutes and serve.

Another option is to cut phyllo sheets lengthwise into strips about 2 inches wide, make 6 cuts. Place 1 tablespoon of spinach mixture at the end of a strip and fold upwards, like a flag, to form triangles. Brush with oil and butter mixture. Place triangles in pan.

Kolokithokeftedes: Zucchini Fritters

yield: 24 (2-inch) fritters

This is Olga's specialty! It's like making zucchini pancakes.

2 medium zucchinis

2 cups flour

1 egg

½ bottle of domestic beer

½ cup parmesan

½ cup kefalograviera, grated (or Swiss)

½ cup feta, grated or crumbled small

½ teaspoon pepper

1 tablespoon flat-leaf parsley, chopped

Grate zucchini on box grater, then salt and drain in colander for 15 minutes. Mix flour, egg, and beer until a thick batter forms. Add ½ cup water to mixture. Adjust water as needed to make a medium batter that is neither runny nor pasty.

Add zucchini and all three cheeses. You want to see a chunky mixture with batter throughout, so add a touch more water if necessary. Add pepper and parsley. Mix thoroughly and drop by tablespoons into hot oil.

Fry until golden in a large sauté pan with about 1 inch of vegetable oil. Remove and drain. Serve warm with Tzatziki Sauce (page 60).

Kourambiedes: Greek Wedding Cookies

yield: 4 dozen

These Greek butter cookies melt in your mouth. My mom called them wedding cookies. They're crescent-shaped and coated with powdered sugar. She had a wonderful "touch" with pasty dough, pies, and cookies.

4 sticks unsalted sweet butter

1 cup powdered sugar

1 egg yolk

¼ teaspoon cinnamon

1 ½ tablespoons bourbon or brandy

½ cup almonds, toasted and chopped

4 - 4½ cups flour, sifted

1 pound powdered sugar for dusting cookies

Melt butter, refrigerate until soft consistency, put in an electric beater, and whip until light and fluffy, about 20 minutes. Add sugar, beat five minutes until smooth. Add egg yolk, cinnamon, clove, and bourbon, and almonds and beat thoroughly.

Pour mixture into a large bowl and add flour, a little at a time until a soft dough is formed that can be handled easily. Pinch off pieces of dough, about 2 tablespoons each, roll into balls, then shape carefully into crescents. Place one inch apart on baking pan and bake at 350 degrees for 30 minutes or until lightly browned.

Handling carefully, place cookies on a flat surface that has been sprinkled with powdered sugar, and sprinkle cookies liberally with powdered sugar while still warm. If the sugar has dissolved, dust again before serving.

Rizogalo: Greek Rice Pudding

yield: 8-10 small ramekins

A rich creamy dessert topped with cinnamon and served cold.

6 tablespoons Arborio rice

1 ½ cups water

6 cups milk

3 tablespoons cornstarch

4 tablespoons warm water

1 cup sugar

1 slice lemon peel

1 tablespoon vanilla

cinnamon

In large saucepan, bring rice and water to a boil. Cover and simmer over medium-low heat until most of the water evaporates, about 10 minutes. Add milk and simmer for about 15 minutes more.

In a cup, dissolve the cornstarch in warm water and add to the rice mixture along with the sugar and lemon peel. Stir constantly over medium-low heat until the mixture turns into a thick and creamy pudding, 15-30 minutes.

Remove lemon peel and stir in vanilla. Pour into individual bowls and sprinkle with cinnamon.

Ouzo Highball

yield: 1

I like to use a tall cylindrical glass.

1 ½ ounces ouzo

8 ounces club soda or water

few ice cubes

Add Ouzo and ice to highball glass, fill with club soda, and enjoy!

Host Your Own Taverna

For setting the table for taverna, I like using an updated lazy susan concept, which is so much easier than passing heavy platters. You can find wooden boards and the necessary mechanics at a home improvement store and then stain or paint them to your liking.

Consider using stemless glasses for easy reaching across the table and small plates—several per person.

Since the food is the center of attention, you don't need floral centerpieces, though I have a pair of fig trees at my home, so I'm partial to using the branches in decorative vases and the leaves as underliners on the platters. The leaves look great under the lamb chops.

Have fun perusing a specialty market for an array of tasty Greek cheeses, olives, and breads to complete your menu.

asian buffet

Asian food naturally lends itself to stations. There's usually quite a bit of chopping involved, though you can prepare just about everything ahead of time. Guests love getting to put together their own assortment of ingredients so it's exactly the way they want. The key to creating Asian-style dinners is to stock your pantry with a few Asian staples such as fish sauce, sweet red chili sauce, hoisin, mirin, dry chilis, and, of course, soy sauce. When entertaining, set yourself up for success and have all the ingredients for each dish pre-measured on a separate tray. Stir fry dishes cook very quickly and are best served immediately. Asian meals are usually healthy, which makes them even more enjoyable to eat, and the food is satisfying without being too heavy.

Ahi Tuna Tartare with Edamame

yield: 3 cups

An all-time favorite! It's wonderful on white porcelain soup spoons or savory edible spoons that can be ordered from **Edibles by Jack,***.*

1 pound sushi/sashimi-grade of ahi tuna, chopped into ¼-inch pieces

1 (12-ounce) bag frozen shelled edamame, blanched

¼ cup chives, chopped

To blanch edamame, bring salted water to a boil in a medium sauce pan and drop edamame into the boiling water for 7 minutes. Drain in a colander and then shock the beans in ice water for 10 minutes. Drain and refrigerate.

Soy-ginger Marinade

3 tablespoons soy sauce

2 tablespoons teriyaki glaze

2 tablespoons pickled ginger

2 tablespoons ginger juice

1 tablespoon mirin

2 tablespoons rice wine vinegar

1 lemon, zest and juice

¼ cup olive oil

1 ½ tablespoons sesame oil

In a blender or food processor mix all ingredients except oils and start to blend. Slowly add oils to produce a thick marinade.

30 minutes before serving, add ¼ cup of marinade to chopped ahi tuna. Place 1-2 tablespoons ahi mixture into Asian spoons, and garnish with chives and a few edamame beans. As an alternative to the spoons, cut a seedless cucumber into 1-inch pieces and scoop out the center with a melon baller to make a small well for ahi mixture. Garnish with seaweed salad, purchased at a local Asian market, if desired.

Thai Flank Steak with Wasabi Cream

yield: 24 pieces

A really tasty hors d'oeuvre. The wasabi cream topping gives it beautiful presentation. This is also a great way to use leftover flank or sirloin steak.

Soy-ginger Marinade

double the ingredients from previous page

Flank Steak

2 cups soy ginger marinade/vinaigrette

2 pounds flank steak

1 cup scallions, chopped

1 cup peanuts, chopped and toasted (optional)

Place flank steak in re-sealable bag with marinade. Let stand at room temperature for 30 to 45 minutes, turning once or twice. While steak is marinating, prep grill to medium-high heat. To cook to medium-rare, grill flank steak on each side for 3 to 5 minutes each side. Transfer to cutting board and tent with foil. Allow to rest for 5 minutes. Slice steak on the bias about ¼-inch thick. Fan out on platter and drizzle over with wasabi cream. Garnish with scallions and peanuts. You can small dice the steak and place in a phyllo shell, as shown.

Wasabi Cream

3 tablespoons wasabi powder

1 cup mayo

Whisk powder into mayo until smooth.

Sushi "Cocktail" with Rice Noodle Salad

yield: 8 cocktails

We've created the "cocktail" in a cosmo glass for a little drama. A Chinese takeout box works well, too. I like to stand the chopsticks up to create a visual effect.

Rice Noodle Salad with Ponzu Sauce

8 sushi rolls or sashimi pieces

pickled ginger

wasabi paste

In each martini glass, add noodle mixture, then top with a piece of sushi or sashimi. Place a small mound of pickled ginger and wasabi paste next to the sushi. Serve with chopsticks.

Ponzu Sauce

yield: 2 cups

3 tablespoons olive oil

3 cloves garlic

½ stalk lemon grass

¼ teaspoon crushed red pepper flakes

1 tablespoon grated ginger

½ cup soy sauce

1 tablespoon mirin

2 tablespoons rice wine vinegar

¼ cup lemon juice

1 cup chicken stock

1 teaspoon nampla (Thai Fish Sauce)

¼ cup finely chopped cilantro

In a stainless steel pot, heat olive oil. Sauté garlic, lemon grass, and chili flakes for 3-4 minutes, then add ginger for 30 seconds. Add remaining ingredients and bring to a hard simmer. Once the heat comes up, turn heat off and let sit for 30-40 minutes. If desired, strain the sauce after cooled.

Rice Noodle Salad

yield: 2 cups

1 (1-pound) package Asian Rice Noodles

1 cup Ponzu Sauce

¼ cup carrots, shredded

¼ cup scallions, sliced on a bias

2-3 tablespoons cilantro, finely chopped (plus extra sprigs for garnish)

1-2 tablespoons white sesame seeds

1-2 tablespoons black sesame seeds

Cook noodles according to package directions and drain. Toss in 1 cup of Ponzu Sauce and chill for 10-15 minutes. Just before assembling, toss in carrots, scallions, chopped cilantro, and sesame seeds. Thoroughly combine noodle mixture.

Thai Noodle Stirfry

yield: 8 cups

Host a fun, interactive station or bar for guests to choose their toppings. Guests will enjoy making a delicious dish without having to cook. Serve the proteins hot as well as the noodles. Everything else can be cold or room temperature. Display the items in this order: noodles, vegetables, proteins, sauces.

3 cups cooked rice noodles or bean thread noodles

1 cup shitake mushrooms, sliced

1 cup Napa cabbage, shredded

1 cup bean sprouts

1 cup green onions, chopped

1 cup carrots, cut into matchsticks

1 cup red bell peppers, cut into matchsticks

3 pounds chicken, cooked and sliced

3 pounds shrimp, cooked

1 cup cilantro, chopped

½ cup soy sauce

1 cup sweet and sour sauce

¼ cup siracha hot sauce

½ cup sesame oil

¼ cup crushed red pepper

Season sliced chicken with salt and pepper and bake. Boil shrimp with lemon juice and salt water. Choose your meats and vegetables and stir fry.

Asian Grilled Chicken Salad

yield: 6 cups

Great for a luncheon or dinner buffet. I like to mix the dressing with the chicken and let it marinate overnight and then mix in the pepper strips on the day of serving. You can use a favorite vinaigrette or a bottled Italian dressing for convenience. The salad is best served at room temperature.

2 pounds boneless chicken breast

1 teaspoon soy sauce

salt and pepper to taste

1 cup red pepper strips

1 cup yellow pepper strips

¼ pound snow peas

½ cup water chestnuts, sliced

½ cup pine nuts, toasted (or almonds)

Season chicken breast with soy sauce, salt, and pepper to taste. Grill-mark chicken for about 8-10 minutes per side. Cook fully and let cool. Cut breast lengthwise into strips. Add vegetables and nuts. Toss with vinaigrette.

Asian Vinaigrette

½ cup Italian dressing

1 tablespoon soy sauce

1 teaspoon sugar

1 teaspoon ground ginger

Combine all ingredients.

Teriyaki Chicken Satay

yield: 12 - 16 pieces

These threaded chicken skewers are moist and delicious. You can use chicken thighs for even juicier meat. It's best to marinate the chicken a day ahead and then skewer—messy but worth the effort. A peanut dipping sauce tops it off. Serve with your favorite peanut dipping sauce.

1 cup teriyaki glaze

¾ cup pickled ginger

4 pieces chicken breast

Chop ginger then mix with teriyaki glaze. Cut strips of chicken (3 to 4 per piece) lengthwise. Marinate chicken for 30-45 minutes. Skewer chicken on long bamboo skewers. Bake at 350 degrees for 15 minutes or until done.

Spicy Thai Chicken

yield: 12 - 16 pieces

This reminds me of the chicken larb dish you get at Asian restaurants. One of my industry friends shared the recipe and I adapted it slightly. We use it to fill mini phyllo pastry shells, and it's also wonderful as a lettuce or cabbage wrap.

½ pound chicken, ground

2 tablespoons vegetable oil

1 clove garlic, chopped

1 tablespoon ginger, peeled and minced

½ teaspoon crushed red pepper flakes, ground to a powder

1 tablespoon soy sauce

⅓ cup ketchup

3 tablespoons brown sugar

salt and pepper to taste

24 phyllo cups

¼ cup dry-roasted peanuts or pine nuts

Heat the oil in a pan over medium high heat. Add chicken, garlic, ginger, and red pepper flakes. Cook for 10-12 minutes or until done, stirring occasionally to break up chicken. Add soy sauce, ketchup, brown sugar, salt, and pepper. Mix well. If the mixture is too chunky, pulse slightly in a food processor. Serve in phyllo shells and garnish with peanuts.

Asian Slaw

yield: 4 cups

So fresh and delicious. The flavors work well with any grilled meat in the summertime.

Dressing

½ cup soy sauce

3 tablespoons grated ginger

⅓ cup rice wine vinegar

3 tablespoons sesame oil

1 cup olive oil

¼ cup lime juice

salt and pepper to taste

Whisk all ingredients together and chill in refrigerator for at least 30 minutes.

Slaw

1 small head green cabbage, shredded

¼ head purple cabbage, shredded

1 bunch scallions, chopped

3 large carrots, peeled and shredded

1 cup fresh bean sprouts

Mix slaw ingredients and add dressing just before serving.

Grilled Shrimp

6 cups water

¼ cup salt

¼ cup lime juice

¼ cup mirin

1 pound of peeled, deveined shrimp (size 16-20)

1 cup olive oil or vegetable oil

½ cup fresh lime juice

1 ½ teaspoons salt

2 tablespoons fresh cilantro, chopped

Combine the water, salt, lime juice, and mirin in a medium size sauce pot. Bring to a boil over medium high heat. Add shrimp, boil for 10-12 minutes or until done. Drain and let cool. In a bowl, combine oil, lime juice, salt, and cilantro and whisk together. Pour oil mixture over cooled shrimp and toss well. Serve over Asian Slaw.

Sesame Seed-encrusted Goat Cheese with Wonton Chips

yield: 16 servings

A lovely visual and a very tasty hors d'oeuvre. It's so simple to do and wows your guests!

Cheese

1 goat cheese log

¼ cup black sesame seeds

¼ cup white sesame seeds

Mix the sesame seeds together and place on parchment paper or big plate. Roll goat cheese log in seed mixture until completely coated. Place in refrigerator until ready to use.

Wontons

4 cups oil for frying

10 wonton wrappers, cut in half diagonally

Heat oil to about 350 degrees and fry wonton halves for 2 minutes on each side, or until golden brown. Cut cheese log into ¼-inch-thick slices and serve on fried wonton chips.

Miso Soup

yield: 8 servings

A Japanese tradition and a wonderful cold-weather friend. It's quick and easy to make and fun to serve in tiny miso soup cups or in soup bowls with porcelain soup spoons.

½ cup dried wakame (seaweed)

¼ cup miso paste (preferably white)

6 cups dashi

3 cups hot water

½ pound soft tofu, cut into ½-inch cubes

¼ cup scallions, thinly sliced

Prepare the broth with dried seaweed, miso paste, dashi, and hot water. Bring mixture to a simmer and a slow boil. Add tofu and continue cooking for 5 minutes. Garnish with scallions.

Saketini

yield: 1 cocktail

A fun, chilled sake drink that goes well with Asian flavors.

½ ounce Absolut Citron

1½ ounce plum sake

splash cranberry juice (optional)

splash grapefruit Juice (optional)

couple drops of Triple Sec

In an ice shaker filled with ice, add all ingredients, shake vigorously, and strain into martini glass. Garnish with a lime wedge.

No Such Thing As Too Many Spoons!

Get some white porcelain spoons. You can do so much with them! Serve them with an Asian soup or use them to serve appetizers and desserts of all varieties, Asian and otherwise. And it's also fun to have edible spoons on hand. My good friend owns Edibles by Jack, which offers Asian spoons in all sorts of savory and sweet flavors. You can find him online to order. Have fun with the presentation. Try mixing a plate of appetizer spoons with a tray of small bowls that have chopsticks sticking out, ready to use. Or what about layering flavors in a cocktail glass? Get creative, guests will appreciate the thoughtful details—and great presentations usually don't take much longer to prepare than ordinary ones, they just require a little planning.

farmer's table

The farm-to-table movement basically refers to food that is ultra-fresh. Produce is harvested at the perfect moment—as opposed to picked early and then left to ripen in a box while it gets shipped from who knows where—and other products are sourced just as fresh as can be. This concept is near and dear to my heart. I have a special appreciation for local fresh produce because my dad had a wholesale produce business for 50 years. When I was growing up, we always had the freshest produce in season. We were doing farm-to-table long before it was chic. But I'm glad it's popular now, because what better way to get excited about creating and sharing wonderful meals than going straight to the source. When you start with fresh and delicious ingredients, the rest is a breeze.

Yellow Tomato Gazpacho

yield: 6 - 8 (1/2 cup) servings

Golden tomatoes are a new twist on a refreshing summertime favorite. You can also use red or green tomatoes. Or try layering all three in a mini pilsner for a unique presentation. The soup is thick enough that the layers will stay intact beautifully.

12 ounces fresh ripe yellow tomatoes, cored

2 cups mango puree

1 ½ teaspoons champagne vinegar

1 ½ teaspoons hot sauce

½ teaspoon ground coriander

1 large cucumber, peeled, seeded, small diced

½ medium red onion, small diced

½ medium white onion, small diced

½ jalapeño, minced

½ small zucchini, small diced

½ small yellow squash, small diced

3 green onions, thinly sliced

¾ teaspoon salt

½ teaspoon black pepper

3 tablespoons cilantro, chopped

¼ cup olive oil

juice of one lime

In large pot, boil enough water to cover tomatoes. Add tomatoes to boiling water for 1-2 minutes to blanch them. Pull them out of the pot and immediately transfer to ice water. Once cool, peel tomatoes and cut in half. Gently squeeze over a fine mesh strainer sitting inside a bowl to remove the seeds. Reserve the juice. Puree tomatoes and combine with reserved tomato juice and all other ingredients. Season to taste with lime juice and cilantro. Chill and serve.

Watermelon and Tomato Salad

yield: 3 cups

A perfect combination of summer fruits, this nutritious salad is great on its own. I like to serve it over baby spinach leaves tossed with balsamic vinegar and extra virgin olive oil.

4 cups seedless watermelon, medium diced

4 cups ripe tomatoes, medium diced

1/3 cup balsamic vinegar

1/4 cup honey slightly warmed

1/4 cup fresh mint, chopped

dash salt

1/2 cup feta, crumbled

Combine watermelon and tomato in large mixing bowl. In a separate, smaller mixing bowl, add balsamic vinegar and warmed honey and whisk till well combined. Pour honey mixture over watermelon mixture. Add chopped mint and dash of salt. Toss till combined well. Garnish with feta and serve immediately. May be served with baby spinach leaves, using the excess liquid from watermelon mixture as dressing.

Caramelized Lemonade

yield: 1 gallon

Who doesn't love fresh lemonade in summer? Thanks to my good friend, Tim Lundy, for sharing this yummy lemonade at one of our conferences. Caramelizing the sugar deepens the flavor and the color, making it even more delicious.

Caramel

4 cups sugar

1 1/2 cups water

In heavy saucepot, add sugar and 1/2 cup water over high heat. Watching caramel constantly, allow sugar to burn and create a golden caramel sauce. Once sugar is caramelized (12-15 minutes), add 1 cup water, being careful not to add water too quickly or it could pop onto your skin. Return caramel syrup to high heat and boil until all caramel is dissolved into caramel syrup.

Lemonade

3 cups fresh lemon juice

3 quarts water

fresh lemon slices

mint sprigs

In pitcher, mix lemon juice with water. Sweeten lemonade with caramel syrup. Mix thoroughly and adjust flavor with additional lemon juice. Garnish with lemon and mint and serve chilled.

Summertime Succotash

yield: 12 servings

Combining the bounty of the farmer's market all in one dish, this succotash is my son Jason's summer specialty. He's demonstrated it several times at our local Pepper Place Market. Other summer vegetables may vary but sweet corn and lima beans are musts for this Native American dish.

½ cup olive oil

2 cups apple smoked bacon, small diced

2 large yellow onions, small diced

½ cup garlic, chopped

2 jalapeño peppers, deseeded and small diced

12 ears corn on the cob, cut off

2 (12 ounce) cans tomato puree

5 cups tomatoes, medium diced

4 cups okra, cut into bite-size pieces

3 cups lima beans (frozen and defrosted, fresh and par-cooked)

4 cups chicken stock

salt and pepper to taste

1 cup parsley, chopped

½ cup fresh basil leaves

Heat a large sauté pan, add olive oil and bacon, and cook for 5 minutes until the bacon has become almost crispy. Add onions, garlic, and jalapeños and cook for 5 minutes. Add fresh corn and sauté for 5-6 minutes. Stir mixture all together for even cooking. Add tomato puree and tomatoes and cook for 10 minutes. Add okra and lima beans and cook for 5 minutes. Add stock, salt, and pepper. Let all ingredients simmer for about 15 minutes then remove from heat. Garnish with parsley and basil.

Okra Casserole with Tomatoes

yield: 8-10 servings

This is one of my dad's specialties. He and my mother both loved to cook but of course when he cooked she was the prep chef! Okra is one of my favorite Southern vegetables. It's so versatile—you can fry it, pickle it, stew it, or bake it. People usually love it or hate it, there's no meeting in the middle, and that's just fine. If you're a fan, this is one delicious way to enjoy it.

2 pounds baby okra

1-2 tablespoons olive oil

1 medium onion, sliced

2 cloves garlic, minced

1 teaspoon salt

½ teaspoon pepper

3-4 ripe tomatoes

1 teaspoon organic chicken base

Wash and trim okra. Sauté onions and garlic in olive oil until translucent and set aside. Sauté whole baby okra in same pan, add salt and pepper. Remove okra and line it up in rows in a 13x9 baking dish. Spread onion and garlic mixture on top of okra. Slice tomatoes in ½-inch rounds. Arrange on top of the okra mixture. Mix teaspoon of organic chicken base, I like Better than Bouillon brand, with 1 cup warm water. Pour over mixture and bake at 350 degrees for 30 minutes.

Easy Greens with Applewood-smoked Bacon

yield: 6 cups

There are tons of possibilities with this one. Substitute the greens for fresh peas, field peas, lady peas, or crowder peas and add a bay leaf and some fresh thyme. Sometimes I'll add fat back or fresh pork lard from the local farmer's market to enhance the flavor.

3-4 slices applewood-smoked bacon

1 medium yellow onion, sliced

dash red pepper flakes or Tabasco

1 bunch greens (turnip, collard, mustard, or kale), chopped

4 cups chicken broth

salt and pepper to taste

In a deep pan, render the bacon, add onions until translucent, then add pepper flakes. Add greens and chicken broth. Cover, bring to a boil, reduce heat, and simmer for 20 minutes. Add salt and pepper to taste, and if greens are bitter, add 1 tablespoon of sugar.

Corn Pudding

yield: 8 servings

Corn pudding goes with everything. It's wonderful with grilled meats, chicken, or fish. I like to use a sweet corn such as Silver Queen but bicolor corn works as well. It may be baked in a buttered casserole dish or in individual ramekins. Be sure to use a water bath when baking.

8 ears sweet corn

1 Vidalia onion, minced

1 quart half and half

4 eggs, whisked

2 tablespoons butter

2 tablespoons brown sugar

salt and white pepper to taste

nutmeg, dash

Preheat oven to 350 degrees. Shave corn off the cobb and use the back of the knife to scrape all the corn milk. Sauté onions in butter until translucent, add corn and half-and-half, and simmer until tender. Season with nutmeg, salt, and pepper. Blend in food processor or blender until smooth and kernels are no longer whole. Whisk in eggs and pour the mixture into a 9x13 buttered casserole dish or ramekins and cover. Place the baking dish into a larger baking dish and add about 1 inch of water to the larger pan. Bake for 45 minutes or until set. Remove cover and bake until crust is golden.

Gardens Cafe Tomato Pie

yield: 1 (9-inch) pie serves 8 people

This is such a delicious way to serve homegrown tomatoes at the height of the summer season. Use any variety of tomatoes available, heirloom, Romas, even teardrops red or gold. We feature this at The Gardens Café midsummer to late summer and always have requests for the recipe!

4 large tomatoes, thinly sliced

½ cup balsamic vinegar

1 yellow onion, sliced

2 cloves garlic, minced

2 tablespoons olive oil

1 nine-inch pie, par-baked

¾ cup real mayonnaise

½ cup grated parmesan

1 cup crumbled feta

3 tablespoons fresh basil, chopped

salt and coarsely ground pepper, to taste

Preheat oven to 350 degrees. Pour vinegar over tomatoes and let them marinate for about 10 minutes, then drain. Season with salt and pepper and add basil. Sauté onions and garlic together in olive oil over medium heat until they are soft and begin to turn golden brown, about 10 minutes. If they begin to stick to the pan, add about 1 tablespoon of water. In a separate bowl, combine mayonnaise and both cheeses. Layer tomato and basil mixture in the bottom of the baked pie shell. Spread sautéed onions on top of tomatoes. Spread mayonnaise and cheese mixture over the top. Bake for 35 minutes or until lightly browned on top.

Heirloom Tomato Stacked Salad with Corn Salsa

yield: 4 servings

This is our summer staple for dinner parties from 10 to 1,000. It holds beautifully and has all the colors of summer. At The Gardens Café we add some whole baby fried okra just before serving.

Corn Salsa

1 cup fresh corn (shaved from cob), cooked

2 jalapeno peppers, seeded and minced (optional)

1 teaspoon sugar

3 tablespoons extra virgin olive oil

3 tablespoons apple cider vinegar

2 cups black eyed peas, cooked

½ cup cilantro, chopped

⅓ cup red onion, diced

⅓ cup red pepper, diced

1 tablespoon lemon juice

In large bowl, add all ingredients and mix well. Let stand for 15 minutes.

Heirloom Tomato Stacks

3 red heirloom tomatoes

2 yellow heirloom tomatoes

salt and pepper to taste

Cut each tomato into ¼-inch-thick slices. Stack the tomatoes in alternating colors: red, yellow, red, yellow, red. Sprinkle stacks with salt and pepper.

Cracked Apple Cider Vinaigrette

1 ½ tablespoons of whole grain mustard

1 tablespoon honey

½ cup apple cider vinegar

1 ½ cups olive oil

Combine all ingredients in a bowl and whisk till well combined.

To assemble: Place the tomato stack on plate. Spoon a heaping ladle of corn salsa over the stack and onto the plate. Pour about 3 tablespoons of vinaigrette over stack and salsa. ***Optional: add a small amount of spring mix or arugula to the plate.

Farmer's Market Pizza

yield: 1 pie

Everyone loves pizza, and what a great meal for the whole family. Any combination of summer vegetables may be used. I like to add some fresh pesto and garnish with fresh basil just before serving.

pizza crust (prebaked or dough)

flour

3 tomatoes, variety of heirloom, Roma, and globe

¼ teaspoon salt

⅛ teaspoon black pepper

½ cup basil pesto (page 46)

2-3 heads of sweet corn, roasted

8 ounces mozzarella, sliced

3 tablespoons basil, chopped

handful of arugula

handful torn kale

½ cup parmesan

½ Vidallia onion, thinly sliced

Preheat oven to 450 degrees. Sprinkle flour onto baking sheet, then lay prebaked pizza crust on top or roll out pizza dough with a rolling pin before placing on the sheet. Spread pesto over pizza crust. Cut roasted sweet corn off the cob and spread it over pesto. Cut tomatoes into slices, laying them on top of the pesto and corn. Sprinkle salt and pepper over tomatoes. Add sliced mozzarella and kale leaves to pizza top. Bake for 15 minutes or until golden brown. Garnish with arugula and parmesan.

Hit the Produce Stands

Wherever you are, whatever the local produce and products, you can just feel the excitement in the air when the farmers' markets open in late spring and run through the summer. Here in Birmingham, markets pop up everywhere—in hospital lobbies, corporate parking decks, downtown parks, community developments, and Pepper Place Market, which is a persoal favorite. Our farmers grow everything from heirloom tomatoes, Silver Queen corn, and okra to rattlesnake beans, lady peas, and Chilton County peaches. In addition to the produce, there are farm-fresh, free-range eggs, pork and beef products, Alabama's McEwen & Sons' organic grits and cornmeal, and other great offerings. Our local chefs strive to preserve our Southern heritage and work with farmers to support locally grown food. So, if you want farm-to-table inspiration, you have to go to the farm—or at least the fabulous markets. Make a day of it!

garden party

In the South, we do bridal teas, we do baby showers, and we do lunch. Ladies love to lunch! I love how special a luncheon sounds and looks and simply is. You say "luncheon" and guests have an idea what to expect—they'll dress up at least a little and maybe a lot, hopefully with a dainty hat or even a fascinator like they do in England. The tea party luncheon concept just always sounds good, whether in the heat of summer on a terrace or in the middle of winter all cozy by the fire. Even though guests know the basics of what to expect, it's always fun to surprise them just a bit, whether it's a new take on an old favorite dish or simply the way you present something. That's what makes the event memorable, well, that and the memories you're making with your dearest friends.

Asparagus Bread Pudding

yield: 8 - 12 servings

We all love sweet bread puddings but this savory one is just divine! It can be served as a side item or even a luncheon entrée as a quiche. Ham or chicken may be added. It goes great with a side salad.

1 pound French bread

1 pound asparagus

12 eggs

4 cups whole milk

2 teaspoons salt

1 teaspoon black pepper, ground

4 cups gruyere or swiss cheese, grated

2 cups Swiss cheese, grated

1 cup parmesan, grated

1/3 cup fresh chives, chopped

1/3 cup fresh parsley, chopped

The night before: Cut French bread into 1 ½-inch pieces and lay it on baking sheets. Let it sit uncovered overnight to let the bread dry out.

The day of: Preheat the oven to 375 degrees. Spray 9×13 dish with pan spray. Cut asparagus into 1 ½-inch pieces. In a medium pot, boil the asparagus until crisp-tender (about 3-4 minutes). Drain asparagus and rinse under cold water. In a large bowl, whisk eggs, milk, salt, and pepper. In a medium bowl, mix cheeses and herbs. Place half of the bread pieces in a glass 9×13 baking dish. Sprinkle half of the asparagus over the bread. Sprinkle half of the cheese and herb mixture over the asparagus. Pour half of the egg mixture over the cheese and herb mixture. Repeat with the remaining ingredients. Let it stand for about 20 minutes. Use a spatula to press on the bread pieces, submerging them into the liquid mixtures. Tent with foil and bake the bread pudding in a water bath by placing the dish that is to be cooked in a bigger, deeper pan. Fill the bigger pan with water until it is about halfway up the side of the center dish. This prevents burning of the food and helps cook dish evenly. Bake the bread pudding for about 45 minutes or until brown and puffy. Uncover and continue baking for another 10 minutes or until golden brown.

Honey Mustard Pecan Chicken Salad

yield: 4 cups

A staple luncheon item on our menu at The Gardens Café. I like to add a dash of fresh lemon juice when mixing. You can vary the nuts—almonds are a great complement, but in the South we think pecans make everything better!

1 ½ pounds chicken, chopped

3 ribs celery, chopped

1 cup toasted pecans, chopped

1 teaspoon salt

1 teaspoon white pepper

½ cup mayonnaise

¼ cup Rothchild raspberry honey mustard

Place skinless chicken breasts in a saucepan and cover with cold water. Bring water to a boil and poach chicken over medium-high heat until chicken reaches an internal temperature of 165 degrees. Drain. Cool chicken. Chop or shred chicken into bite-sized pieces. In a bowl, mix chicken with all of the remaining ingredients.

Carrot Ginger Soup

yield: 8 servings

I like to serve this at The Gardens Café in the spring and fall using organic carrots from our local purveyor. We've dressed it up in a martini glass for a black tie dinner and served it with a beet salad for a "not your usual soup and salad" dinner.

1 tablespoon olive oil

2 medium onions, sliced

¼ cup fresh ginger, peeled and grated

3 cups chicken stock

4 large carrots, roughly cut in even pieces

salt and white pepper

2-4 tablespoons heavy cream

In large saucepot, heat olive oil over low heat, and sauté onion until translucent. Add grated ginger and sauté for an additional two minutes. Increase the heat and add the chicken stock and carrots. Simmer over medium heat until carrots are tender. Season with salt and pepper. Puree. Finish with a small amount of cream.

Herb-roasted Chicken Over Fava Bean Pesto on Bruschetta

yield: 12-15 servings

This is a simple hors d'oeuvre which is lovely in the springtime. The bright green pesto is a beautiful background for the slice of chicken.

Chicken and Bruschetta

1 ½ pounds boneless skinless chicken breast

1 artisan bread loaf (rosemary boule or French baguette), cut into ½-inch slices

salt and pepper

olive oil

micro greens or parmesan for garnish

Heat grill or grill pan to medium-high heat. Place bread slices on ungreased grill for 5 minutes on each side. Remove and brush with olive oil and sprinkle with salt and pepper. Set bread slices aside and spray grill with non-stick cooking spray. Sprinkle chicken breasts with salt and pepper and place on grill. Thickness will determine cooking time, which may average 8-10 minutes on each side. Internal temperature should reach 165 degrees. Slice chicken into thin slices on the bias.

To assemble, generously spread Fava Bean Pesto on bread, lay chicken breast slices on top, and garnish.

Fava Bean Pesto

yield: 2 cups

Fava beans have a wonderful flavor, though if you can't get them locally, shelled edamame is a great substitute, just blanch the frozen edamame for a few minutes.

3 cups fava beans, shelled (or edamame)

¼ cup olive oil

¼ cup parmesan, grated

salt and pepper to taste

½ cup basil pesto

½ cup parsley

In saucepot, bring salted water to a boil and fava beans until tender, about 5-8 minutes. Shock in ice and cold water bath. In a food processor, blend beans, olive oil, parmesan, salt, pepper, and parsley until smooth. You may need more olive oil to achieve a spreadable consistency

Encrusted Tea Sandwiches

yield: 32 pieces

For special allergy considerations, use finely chopped parsley instead of nuts. I love this presentation adapted from Martha Stewart. It makes simple tea sandwiches so much lovelier.

4 cups almonds, sliced and toasted

1 cup mayonnaise

2 cups parsley, chopped

½ cup honey

Honey Mustard and Pecan Chicken Salad (page 99)

Pimento Cheese (page144)

2 loaves of bread, white or wheat

Spread Chicken Salad on 4 pieces of bread and top with another piece of bread. Spread Pimento Cheese on 4 pieces of bread and top with another piece of bread. Cut crusts off sandwiches. Cut each whole sandwich into four triangle pieces. In a bowl, combine mayo and honey and mix well. Chop or crush the toasted almonds slightly. Spread mayo mixture on the outside of the sandwiches and dip in the crushed almonds or chopped parsley as shown on left. Serve chilled.

Watermelon Cubes with Balsamic Syrup

yield: 24 servings

So simple and totally refreshing. The sweetness of the balsamic blends nicely with the melon.

1 small seedless watermelon, cut in 1-inch cubes

1 cup balsamic vinegar

In a small saucepan, cook the balsamic vinegar until it is reduced by half, or until thick and drizzles easily. Being careful not to overcook and burn.

Using a melon baller, cut out a divot from the center of the watermelon, being careful to not go all the way through.

Place the watermelon cubes on a tray, drizzle a small amount of the balsamic reduction in the watermelon.

Gougéres (French Cheese Puffs)

yield: 24

Gougéres in French cuisine are baked savory choux pastry made of choux dough mixed with cheese. They're classically made with gruyere cheese, but we've adapted them and added parmesan instead. They may have sweet or savory fillings or stand alone. Have them on a cookie sheet ready to bake as guests arrive. The aroma is so divine your guests won't be able to wait to enjoy them.

$^2/_3$ cup water

4 tablespoons butter

$^1/_2$ teaspoon salt

1 cup flour

4 eggs

$^1/_4$ cup parmesan, grated

$^1/_2$ cup swiss cheese, grated

$^1/_2$ teaspoon freshly ground pepper

Bring water to boil with butter and salt. As soon as water boils, lower heat and add flour all at once. Cook the paste, beating it briskly with a wooden spoon, until the mixture forms a ball and leaves the sides of the pan clean. Remove pan from heat and put in a stand mixer. Beat in the eggs, one at a time, incorporating each egg thoroughly before adding the next. Add both cheeses and pepper. Using piping bag, pipe 1 $^1/_2$-inch circles onto parchment-lined sheet pan. Bake at 375 for 15-18 minutes until golden brown.

Lemon Buttermilk Tart

yield: 1 (10-inch) pie or 4 (4-inch) shells

Lemon desserts are always refreshing after a meal, especially on a warm spring or summer day. I love this one!.

4 eggs

1 ⅓ cups sugar

¼ cup buttermilk

2 tablespoons cornmeal

3 tablespoons lemon juice

pinch of salt

1 lemon, zested and juiced

nutmeg

1 (10-inch) frozen pie shell or 4 (4-inch)
pie shells

Preheat oven to 450 degrees. Beat eggs lightly and add sugar. Stir in salt, buttermilk, cornmeal, and butter until smooth. Add lemon zest and juice. Fill a 10-inch, partially baked tart shell. Grate a little bit of nutmeg over top of filling. Place pie on sheet pan in oven. Immediately reduce oven temperature to 325 degrees and bake for about 35 minutes, until custard is just set in center. Do not allow filling to puff.

Spring Pea Soup

yield: 8 - 10 servings

A delightful luncheon soup, served cold. It's also called Potage St. Germaine, which refers to any soup made with fresh green peas or greens. It's delicious with a crisp white wine.

pea mixture

1 (1-pound) package fresh or frozen sweet English peas

½ cup water

1 shallot, chopped

6-8 leaves Boston lettuce

1 tablespoon butter

¼ teaspoon salt

In saucepot, boil peas in ½ cup of water with shallot, lettuce, butter, and salt for about 10 minutes or until the peas are tender. Puree the mixture and set aside.

potato mixture

1 large yellow onion, chopped

3 tablespoons butter

3 tablespoons flour

4 cups hot chicken stock or water

1 large potato, peeled and sliced

1 ½ teaspoon salt

In large pot, sauté onion in butter for about 10 minutes. Do not brown. Blend in flour and stir for about 1 minute. Blend in 1 cup of the hot chicken stock. Once it is completely blended, stir in the remaining 3 cups. Add the sliced potato and salt and simmer for about 20 minutes or until the potatoes are soft. Puree the mixture and return it to the pot.

finishing mixture

½ cup milk

¼ cup heavy cream or sour cream

Stir the pea mixture into the potato mixture and add milk to thin. Just before serving, stir in cream. Serve chilled or hot.

This floating glass beverage table was inspired by Meryl Snow

Sgroppino

yield: 2 (6-ounce) servings

We sometimes call this drink "Heaven" because it's so yummy. It's a classic drink from Venice that's served as a digestive between the meal and dessert. Sgroppino is best made with lemon sorbet, not ice cream. In Venice, your waiter might make sgroppino at your table by beating the sorbet and prosecco into a mixture as fluffy as whipped snow. I've heard this is a favorite of Julia Roberts.

2 ½ scoops lemon sorbet

4 tablespoons prosecco

4 tablespoons vodka

2 tablespoons whipped cream

Blend the sorbet and liquid ingredients.

Stage a Luncheon with Style

When guests arrive, you always want to offer them a drink, cool in the spring and summer, warm in the fall and winter. A sparkling beverage is a nice touch any time of year. If you make it just a little bit fancy, you're setting a tone of excitement right from the beginning. Whether you're indoors or out, it's ideal to host the party somewhere with good views of nature. Set the tables with an extra layer of linens so the look is sumptuous and feminine. Top them with groupings of apples or other seasonal fruit, moss, and other nature-inspired elements. Decorate the whole setting with lots of flowers, paying particular attention to the centerpieces, since they'll be enjoyed throughout the afternoon.

Inspired by Martha Stewart, at our pink and green bridesmaid's luncheon we made a cornice of rosebuds by hot-gluing the heads onto foam board cut to fill the corner. We tied monogrammed chiffon "take home" scarves on each guest's chair. After all, girls love anything monogrammed!

pasta party

Everybody loves pasta. Everybody. So when you invite people to a pasta party, they'll come. And they'll have a marvelous time even if you only serve the basics. But it's always nice to do something a little different, to make your guests feel all the more special. Serve a wide variety of pasta dishes in creative ways. Start with an antipasta platter, maybe try your hand at homemade pasta, and go all-out with the sauces. Marinara, cream, pesto, garlic and oil, vegetable, meat—it's incredible what the sauce alone does to the dish. Of course pasta stations work great for any size of party so that guests can choose their own add-ins—meat, seafood, a bounty of veggies, or a little of everything. Whether you prefer to roast, grill, or sauté, adding a wide variety of vegetables to the presentation immediately takes the meal from ordinary to extraordinary.

Prosecco
with Limoncello

yield: 2 cocktails

Limoncello is traditionally used as a digestive after a meal. I've paired it with bubbly prosecco, added raspberries, and used it as an aperitif at the beginning of an evening. Adding fresh raspberries and mint makes it a perfect summer cocktail. It is just as delicious with just the prosecco and limoncello year-round. Be sure to add the prosecco just before serving.

10 fresh raspberries

2 sprigs fresh mint

4 ounces cold prosecco

2 ounces limoncello liqueur, cold

Chill glasses. Add 5 raspberries in each glass. Gently smash mint leaves and add to glasses, followed by limoncello and then prosecco.

Antipasta Skewers

yield: 20

Easy to do and colorful, too! Any combination of savory salamis or cheeses works well for this hors d'oeuvre. You can alternate with roasted red pepper pieces and marinated artichoke hearts.

20 artichoke hearts, quartered

20 Kalamata olives, pitted

20 roasted red pepper slices

I pound fresh mozzarella, cut into ¾-inch cubes

20 grape tomatoes

½ cup basil pesto (page 46)

20 bamboo skewers

Keep each item in a separate container, add a couple of spoonfuls of pesto to each container, and toss to coat completely. On a skewer, place one piece each of artichoke, olive, mozzarella, and tomato. Repeat on remaining skewers. Refrigerate until ready to serve.

Creamy Fettuccini with Pancetta and Leeks

yield: 6 servings

A creamy pasta that's light and delicious, this is a standalone dish that adds a bit of decadence on a pasta buffet.

1 pound fettuccini or tagliatelle, cooked al dente

2 tablespoons olive oil

1 tablespoon unsalted butter

1 cup pancetta, diced

2 medium leeks, white tops sliced

kosher salt

¾ cup heavy cream

2 teaspoons fresh thyme, chopped

1 teaspoon fresh rosemary, chopped

1 teaspoon fresh garlic, chopped

½ cup water

1 cup parmesan, finely grated

Cook pasta until al dente and reserve 2 cups of liquid. In a large heavy pot, heat oil and butter over medium heat. Add pancetta and cook, stirring often, until fat is rendered and pancetta is crisp, 5-8 minutes. Add leeks, garlic, and salt. Increase heat to medium-high and cook, stirring often, until leeks begin to brown, 5-8 minutes. Add cream, thyme, rosemary, garlic, and water. Bring to a boil, reduce heat, and simmer, stirring occasionally, until sauce is thickened and coats the back of a spoon, 5-8 minutes. Add pasta, parmesan, and 1 cup pasta-cooking liquid to sauce and stir to coat. Increase heat to medium and continue stirring, adding more cooking liquid until sauce coats pasta.

Chicken Artichoke Lasagna

yield: 12 servings

This spin on lasagna has been a staple for us. It's a wonderful "fireside" or Sunday night supper. It is ideal for entertaining groups since it can be made ahead and frozen. Just defrost, cook, and serve with a Caesar salad and crusty bread.

²/₃ cup butter

¹/₃ cup flour

1 teaspoon salt

¹/₈ teaspoon white pepper

½ teaspoon garlic

¼ teaspoon ground nutmeg

3 cups milk

2 pounds boneless chicken breast, cooked and shredded

2 cans water-packed artichokes, drained and shredded

1 teaspoon dried thyme

9-12 lasagna noodles, cooked

1 ½ cups parmesan, grated

9-12 slices fresh mozzarella

In saucepan over medium heat, make a roux by melting butter and stirring in flour. Season with salt, pepper, garlic, and ground nutmeg. Once it cooks to a smooth consistency for approximately 5 minutes, slowly add milk. Bring just up to a boil and then lower to a simmer for another 5 minutes, until sauce is thick. Take sauce off heat and check seasoning.

Preheat oven to 350 degrees. In a 13x9 baking dish, layer 3 pasta sheets, a third of the chicken, a third of the artichokes, a third of the roux, and sprinkle with parmesan. Repeat to use remaining ingredients and finish the top with mozzarella. Cover and bake for 35 minutes, then uncover and cook an additional 10 minutes, until bubbly around the edges.

Penne with Tomato Cream Sauce

yield: 6 servings

We've served this dish as a buffet item to large groups. Chicken strips or cooked shrimp may be added to make it an entrée.

2 medium garlic cloves

6 tablespoons olive oil

2 (28-ounce) cans San Marzano whole tomatoes

salt and pepper to taste

1 teaspoon red chili pepper flakes

1 pound dry penne pasta

1 cup heavy cream

12 sprigs parsley

1-2 cups parmesan, finely grated

Roughly chop garlic. In medium saucepan, heat oil over medium heat. When oil is warm, add garlic and sauté for 3 minutes, being careful not to burn. Add canned tomatoes and cook for 20 minutes. Add salt and pepper to taste, then add chili flakes. Pass sauce mixture through a food mill or food processor until smooth and pour into large skillet. Reduce heat to low and let the sauce simmer. Meanwhile, bring pot of water to boil for penne. While pasta is cooking, coarsely chop parsley and set aside. Drain pasta when it is al dente (approximately 10 minutes) and pour into skillet with tomato sauce. Increase heat to medium and sauté for 1 minute. Add cream and mix until pasta is coated. Pour into a serving dish and garnish with parsley and parmesan. Serve hot.

Veal Meatballs

yield: 24 meatballs

This is my favorite meatball dish—very light because of the cream or ricotta. I like to make a large batch and freeze. Meatballs are wonderful to have on hand. I love Ty's idea of a "meatballs and movie" theme night!

2 pounds veal, ground

1 pound sweet Italian sausage

1 medium onion

2 cloves garlic

½ cup panko

1 cup parmesan

2 teaspoons basil

½ teaspoon black pepper

4 eggs

½ cup half-and-half or ricotta cheese

3-4 cups red sauce

2 ounces basil leaves, chiffonaded

Place meat in a bowl and mix well. Add finely chopped or processed onion and garlic and mix well. Add remaining ingredients and mix well. If mixture is too wet, add panko until desired consistency is achieved. With oiled hands, form in 1- or 1 ½-inch balls. Bake in convection oven at 350 degrees for approximately 10 minutes to par-bake. Finish in a red sauce. Garnish with basil.

Cavatelli with Bolognese

yield: 4-6 servings

This is my favorite meat sauce. I always make this in a larger batch and freeze the sauce for later use. Cavatelli, ziti, small shell, or mini penne will hold the chunky sauce best.

1 pound cavatelli pasta

3 tablespoons olive oil

1 sweet onion, finely chopped

3 celery stalks, finely chopped

2 carrots, finely chopped

5 cloves garlic, minced

salt and pepper, pinch

¼ pound pancetta or applewood-smoked bacon

1 pound ground veal or pork

1 pound bulk Italian sausage (spicy or mild)

1 cup burgandy wine

2 (14-ounce) cans San Marzano whole tomatoes, crushed by hand

3 sprigs fresh thyme

2 bay leaves

¼ - ½ teaspoon crushed red pepper (optional)

Cook pasta until al dente. In large pan, heat oil to medium and add vegetables to sweat until translucent, about 5 minutes, and season with salt and pepper. Add meat and cook until browned but not done completely. Add wine and cook until half of the liquid is gone. Add tomatoes, thyme, bay leaves, and red pepper. Reduce to a simmer and cook for 1 hour. Serve over pasta.

Tiramisu

yield: 8 cosmo glasses

I like to use Genoise or pound cake instead of traditional lady fingers. Bonnie started doing this when we needed it for large groups because it holds up better. When I had it in Italy served unmolded and topped with a chocolate ganache, I definitely enjoyed seconds.

Genoise

2 ½ cups flour

2 cups sugar, divided use

12 eggs

1½ slicks of butter, melted

2 teaspoons vanilla extract

Sift flour and ½ cup sugar three times. Whisk eggs and 1 ½ cups sugar over water bath until warm, then beat with a mixer on high until ribbon consistency. Fold flour mix into egg mix in 3 additions. Temper in butter and vanilla. Spread evenly on a greased half-sheet pan or cookie sheet. Bake at 350 degrees to golden.

Filling

¾ teaspoon gelatin

10 tablespoons marsala

3 egg yolks

½ cup sugar

1 cup cream

8 ounces mascarpone, room temperature

1 cup coffee, black

dark cocoa powder, for garnish

In small bowl, sprinkle gelatin on top of ¼-cup of marsala, reserve. In medium bowl, combine yolks, sugar, and remaining marsala over a water bath and heat/whisk like making a sabayon (soft peaks). Remove and place in a mixer bowl with whip attachment and whip until cool to the touch. Chill. Whip the cream to stiff peaks, reserve. Gradually stir egg mixture into soft mascarpone, followed by whipped cream. Heat gelatin mixture to dissolve. Temper into cream mixture. Use immediately. Take the baked and cooled Genoise cake and cut into 8 small rounds (the size that fits the bottom of a cosmo or martini glass) and 8 medium-sized rounds (the size that fits about halfway up the glass). Coffee-soak the cake rounds by either pouring a teaspoon or a tablespoon of coffee—depending on the size of the cake layer—directly on the cake or quickly dipping the cake in coffee. In each cosmo glass, layer a small dollop of cream mixture, a small coffee-soaked cake round, cream, large coffee-soaked cake layer, and cream. Garnish with cocoa powder.

Serving Options Galore

I like to serve pasta parties family-style with bowls placed directly on the table for a group of 6-8. If you're entertaining a crowd, set up a pasta bar—as many kinds of pasta, sauces, and toppings as you'd like. Keep your sauces warm in a crock pot or chafer. Cook the pasta al dente, then drain it and add a tablespoon of olive oil to keep it from sticking. Toppings can include Italian sausage, meatballs, roasted vegetables, chicken, or shrimp. Add a green salad of arugula and serve it with a bottle each of extra-virgin olive oil and aged balsamic. And, of course, lots of freshly grated parmesan! Complement the display with whole vegetables like eggplant, zucchini, artichokes, and tons of tomatoes for great color and texture. A fun desert is chocolate fettucini with fresh raspberries and whipped cream.

dinner party

Don't be daunted by the idea of a formal dinner party, be inspired! If you're going it alone, keep it simple. Keep. It. Simple. Focus on the parts that are most important to you and unabashedly outsource the rest. Start with dessert. Choose something that sounds fun and make it well ahead of time so that you can enjoy the process of baking it. If you're doing a pie and the crust is daunting to you, just buy it readymade and make the filling from scratch. To make life a little easier, and make dinner a little more interactive, you can even do a mixture of serving the entrée plated and serving the sides family-style. Maybe bring out the food in waves to carry on the evening's momentum and keep people anticipating what will come next. Of course, there's always the option of setting up the dinner buffet-style and have guests design their own plate.

Bibb Lettuce Salad with Feta and Strawberries

yield: 2-3 servings

A refreshing choice for all occasions. We like to serve it with either champagne vinegar or lemon vinaigrette. In spring, it's nice to add edible flowers to create the look of a bouquet.

1 head bibb lettuce, washed, cored, kept whole

¼ cup strawberries, sliced

¼ cup feta, crumbled

¼ cup almonds, sliced and toasted

Lemon Vinaigrette

2 tablespoons lemon juice

½ teaspoon lemon zest

½ teaspoon Dijon mustard

¼ teaspoon sea salt

½ teaspoon sugar

¼ cup extra virgin olive oil

In small bowl, whisk lemon juice, lemon zest, mustard, salt, and sugar until sugar is dissolved. Add olive oil in a steady stream until blended.

Place lettuce in center of plate; it may tilt slightly and that is fine. Sprinkle cheese and strawberries over lettuce and on the plate, avoiding the rim. Drizzle with vinaigrette just before serving.

Asparagus Salad with Corn Timbale

yield: 2-3 servings

A delightful presentation for a first course. The rectangular plate adds more drama to the look. I like to serve the vinaigrette on the side in a small glass.

16 large asparagus spears

1 golden beet, roasted and diced

1 cup fresh mache, arugula, or salad greens

6 ounces lump crab (optional)

4 tablespoons basil pesto (page 46)

1 cup basil vinaigrette

Corn Timbale (page 90 - Corn Pudding)

4 toasted crostinis (page 48)

Basil Vinaigrette

1 pod shallot, finely chopped

2 tablespoons white balsamic vinegar

6 tablespoons extra virgin olive oil

1 tablespoon fresh basil, chopped

salt and pepper to taste

Combine all ingredients in small bowl and wisk well.

Prepare soufflé and let cool. Blanch asparagus in boiling water for 3 minutes, remove, and put in ice water bath. Roast and finely dice beet. Place corn timbale in center of plate. Place 2 asparagus spears on either side of plate, crisscrossed. Arrange beets around asparagus. Garnish with greens. Place corn timbale in center of plate. Top corn timbale with lump crabmeat. Put a small amount of dressing into a shot glass and arrange on plate. Serve chilled. Add the toasted crostini spread with basil pesto.

Oatmeal Stout Pot Roast

yield: 6-8 servings

Pot roast is the ultimate comfort food, and with this recipe you can transform a basic dinner party into a divine one! Allan added the oatmeal stout beer, which tenderizes the roast even more. Use leftovers for sliders with blackberry onion jam.

3 tablespoons olive oil

2 tablespoons butter

3 tablespoons flour

1 (5-pound) chuck roast

salt and pepper to taste

1 (12-ounce) bottle Oatmeal Stout Beer or Guinness

6 large carrots, cut into ½-inch pieces

2 large sweet onions, cut into large diced pieces

3 stalks celery, cut into ½-inch pieces

2 quarts beef stock

2-3 sprigs thyme and rosemary

2 dried bay leaves

2-3 cloves garlic

Preheat oven to 350 degrees. In Dutch oven with lid, heat oil and butter on stovetop on medium-high heat. Flour the roast on all sides, then sprinkle with salt and pepper. Make slits in the roast and insert garlic pods in fatty crevices. Add roast to Dutch oven and sear on all sides. Remove roast from pot. Add beer and deglaze by scraping around the pot. Return meat to pan and add stock. Add thyme, rosemary, bay leaves, and garlic. Bring to a gentle simmer. Cover with lid and transfer to oven. Cook for 3-4 hours, until fork-tender. Add vegetables to pot. Add more beef stock if needed. Cook another 30 minutes until vegetables are fork-tender.

Roasted Tri-Color Potatoes

yield: 8-10 servings

To serve as an hors d'oeuvre, just cut in half lengthwise, bake, then top with sour cream and a half teaspoon of caviar. Of course, they also make a colorful buffet side item to complement beef, lamb, or chicken.

1 pound purple/blue fingerling potatoes

1 pound yellow/orange fingerling potatoes

1 pound white fingerling potatoes

2 tablespoons rosemary, chopped

1 tablespoon thyme, chopped

salt and pepper to taste

2-3 tablespoons olive oil

Cut potatoes in half lengthwise. Blanch each type of potatoes separately and cool. In a bowl, mix remaining ingredients and toss gently. Spread out on a sheet pan and bake at 350 degrees for 15-20 minutes or until crisp and golden brown. Serve warm.

Cedar Plank Salmon with Soy Ginger Glaze

yield: 8-10 party-style with party rye, 4-6 dinner buffet-style

Serve it hot or cold, tastes great either way. We usually present it on a wood plank served with horseradish mashed potatoes and asparagus. Wild rice and cranberry scones also make a beautiful autumn dinner. For a simple sauce, try tarragon mayonnaise flavored with apple butter and mirin.

1 side fresh Atlantic salmon, pin bones out, skin off

1 cedar plank, approximately 20x6, sanded on both sides and all edges

canola oil

2 cups soy sauce

2 tablespoons ground ginger

1 cup brown sugar

salt and pepper

In medium saucepot over medium-high heat, combine soy sauce, ginger, and brown sugar. Reduce mixture until thickened. Be careful not to let mixture boil over. Preheat oven to 350 degrees. Brush the cedar plank will canola oil. Trim salmon of any excess fat, transfer to plank, and season with salt and pepper. Drizzle some of the soy glaze on top, reserving some for basting. Roast in oven for 10-15 minutes until fork tender.

Praline Cheesecake

yield: 1 (9-inch) cake, 12-16 slices

Definitely a decadent ending to a meal. Make it ahead and sit back and enjoy with your guests!

Crust

3 cups graham cracker crumbs

1 cup sugar

1 stick butter, melted

Combine all ingredients and pack down on the bottom of a greased, spring form pan. Set aside.

Praline Mixture

6 tablespoons butter

½ cup brown sugar

⅓ cup pecans, pieces

In small saucepot, combine butter and brown sugar. Heat on medium-high and stir until mixture bubbles and sugar is dissolved. Don't let it overcook and thicken, you want it pourable. Add pecans.

Filling

4 (8-ounce) packages cream cheese

1 ¼ cups granulated sugar

5 eggs

In mixer, blend cream cheese and sugar until smooth. Add eggs one at a time until incorporated. Pour into pan over graham cracker crust. Spoon praline mixture over filling. Bake in water bath at 300 degrees until set.

Tawny Port Wine Flan with Valencia Orange

yield: 6 (6-ounce) ramekins

Beautiful and wonderfully light and refreshing. The perfect ending for a dinner party. It's as lovely tasting as it looks!

Caramelized Syrup

½ cup sugar

½ cup boiling water

In saucepan, add sugar and water. Cook down until consistency is like maple syrup. Pour 2 tablespoons of syrup into bottom of each ramekin. Tilt ramekin in all directions to line bottom. Let cool before adding custard.

Custard

1 ½ cups half-and-half

1 ½ cups heavy cream

2 teaspoons orange zest

¾ cup sugar

3 whole eggs

3 egg yolks

3 tablespoons tawny port wine

2 Valencia oranges

Preheat oven to 350 degrees. In a heavy saucepan, bring half-and-half, heavy cream, and orange zest to a simmer. In a bowl, beat sugar into eggs and egg yolks with a whisk until frothy. Gradually pour 1 cup of cream mixture in a thin stream of droplets into yolks. Add back into saucepan and heat, stirring constantly for 1 minute. Remove from heat, stir in wine, and strain the mixture through a fine-meshed sieve and pour about ½ cup to ¾ cup into the caramel-lined molds. Set ramekins in a 13x9 baking dish, and pour boiling water halfway up on sides to create a bain marie, water bath. Place on bottom rack of preheated oven, reduce heat to 325 degrees, and bake for 25 minutes or until knife comes clean when inserted in the center. Chill. When ready to serve, run a dinner knife around the edges and invert onto individual dessert plates. Garnish with zested Valencia orange peel and segments.

Tables for 5,000

If you're feeding more people than will fit at your dining room table, have it catered! By us, by anyone. Formal dinner parties are what caterers do best. You can be the ultimate hostess and greet your guests, offer them a refreshing aperitif. Using your serving pieces would also personalize a catered affair at home. And needless to say, having someone help with the cleanup makes you feel like a guest at your own event.

As far as centerpieces, think collections of varying sizes in votives and candlesticks. A mix and match of metals is lovely and adds more interest to the table setting. The collected look is easy and very much in vogue now. Mixing in florals with candles is lovely, though make sure guests can see above and around your design.

autumn fare

Fall is my all-time favorite time of the year. Bright, sunny, crisp days with finally no humidity makes me feel great to be alive. Finally the heat is passing and we see the rustic palate of changing leaves grace us with new beauty. So many foods bring back memories of autumn weekends, football—of course, we're in the South—family traditions, and holiday fun. When autumn is in full swing, our thoughts turn to harvest festivals and fireside suppers. Family times with upcoming holidays all revolve around being at the table together. Everyone has their favorite way to prepare certain dishes so it's fun to mix things up once in a while—get the folks who don't usually like sweet potatoes to give them another chance or coax the traditionalists into falling in love with an unusual seasoning combination.

Paella in a Pumpkin

yield: 8 servings

Paella is a wonderful hearty dish for entertaining. It's colorful and can be served straight from a paella pan or in a seasonal roasted pumpkin (see next page) bowl! You can mix and match any shellfish with sausage and chicken, which can be grilled or sautéed before combing into the dish. We've prepared this for 300 guests for a black tie gala for the ballet with a Don Quixote theme. The event was held in a major upscale retail store and we had to work out of the supply rooms!

Chicken

6 chicken thighs with skin on

2 medium-sized chicken breasts

1 tablespoon paprika

2 teaspoons oregano, chopped

2 teaspoons parsley, chopped

Kosher salt and freshly ground pepper to taste

Marinate chicken with paprika, oregano, parsley, salt, and pepper. Rub herb marinade on chicken and roast at 400 degrees for 20 minutes or until done. Let cool and shred or chop chicken.

Saffron Rice

4 cups short-grain white rice

3 cups warm water

3 cups clam juice

1 heaping teaspoon saffron threads

Boil water and clam juice. Add rice and saffron, cover, and cook for 30 minutes or until al dente.

Spanish Paella

¼ cup extra-virgin olive oil

1 Spanish onion, diced

4 garlic cloves, crushed

4 red bell peppers, diced

1 (15-ounce) can whole tomatoes, drained and hand-crushed

1 stalk celery, diced

2 Andouille sausages, thickly sliced

chicken, see above

1 pound jumbo shrimp, peeled and de-veined

1 dozen mussels (or clams)

1 cup white wine

4 cups clam juice

saffron rice, see above

1 bunch flat-leaf parsley leaves, chopped, reserve some for garnish

lemon wedges for serving

3 tablespoons butter

salt and pepper to taste

In large pan, heat olive oil. Make a sofrito by sautéing the onions, garlic, red pepper, tomatoes, and celery. Cook for 2-3 minutes on medium heat. Add Andouille sausage, chicken, shrimp, and mussels. Cook for 4 minutes and deglaze pan with 1 cup white wine and 3 cups clam juice. Add cooked saffron rice, cover, and let simmer for 15 minutes. Add parsley and butter. Add salt and pepper to taste. Dish into 6 bowls and serve with lemon wedges.

Roasted Pumpkin Bowl

1 personal or baker's pumpkin

Cut top off the pumpkin and keep the stem. Clean out pumpkin with a spoon and wash. Liberally oil the inside and outside of the pumpkin and pumpkin top. Roast in the oven at 275 degrees for 30 minutes or until tender but still keeps its shape. Let cool. Use as a bowl for Spanish Paella or Shrimp Corn Chowder.

Shrimp and Corn Chowder

yield: 6-8 servings

This is a hearty soup that can stand alone for lunch or dinner. Serve in a roasted pumpkin serving bowl or individual bowls. Crusty bread is the perfect complement.

4 tablespoons butter

3 teaspoons chopped garlic

3 small onions, chopped

1 cup Riesling wine

4 cups chicken stock

1 ½ teaspoon crushed red pepper

½ teaspoon ground cumin

2 Idaho potatoes, quartered

6-8 small red potatoes, halved

1 ½ pounds medium shrimp, peeled and deveined

3 cups frozen corn kernels

1 cup half-and-half

¼ cup fresh lime juice

¼ cup cilantro, chopped

1 cup cornstarch

1 cup cold water

In a pot over moderate heat, melt 2 tablespoons butter with 1 teaspoon garlic and half of the amount of onion. Sauté, stirring occasionally, for about 4 minutes. Add wine and stock; simmer, stirring occasionally until liquid is reduced to 4 cups, about 20 minutes. Strain stock, discard solids, and set broth aside. In the same pot, melt remaining butter over moderate heat. Add remaining onion, crushed red peppers, and cumin; cook, stirring occasionally until onion is tender, about 3 minutes. Add remaining garlic and cook, stirring occasionally for 1 minute. Add broth, and potatoes; simmer, stirring occasionally until potatoes are fork-tender, adding more water to cover potatoes if necessary, about 20 minutes. Mash some of the Idaho potatoes with a fork to thicken soup. If the soup still needs thickening, make a cornstarch slurry with the cornstarch and cold water mixed well. Slowly add to the soup and continue to cook until thickened. Stir in shrimp and corn; simmer until shrimp are just cooked through, about 3 minutes. Add half-and-half, juice, and cilantro. Season to taste with salt and pepper. Ladle soup into bowls and serve with lime wedges.

Coq au Vin

yield: 6 servings

There are variations of coq au vin using red wine but I've always use a dry white. I've been making this recipe for years at home and my family always loves it. It's definitely one of the children's comfort foods. We've added it to our fall menus for buffet dinners or in our Gardens Café for lunch. I like to use chicken leg quarters mostly with some breast on the bone. The dark meat is always more flavorful in a braised dish. Serve with a green vegetable or salad and crusty bread.

3 slices of lean bacon

3 tablespoons butter

3 small onions

2 large carrots

6 new potatoes

½ teaspoon salt

½ teaspoon pepper

1 tablespoon olive oil

2 ½ - 3 pounds of chicken

3 tablespoons flour

3 cups chicken stock

¼ cup brandy

1 cup dry white wine or vermouth

1 tablespoon tomato paste

¼ teaspoon thyme

1 bay leaf

1 clove of garlic, minced

Portobello mushrooms (optional)

Preheat the oven to 350 degrees. Simmer 3 slices of lean bacon in a quart of water for 10 minutes, then drain on a paper towel. In skillet, sauté the bacon pieces in 2 tablespoons of butter, until it is lightly browned. Pour bacon into a roasting pan or Dutch oven.

Season chicken with salt and pepper. Add 1 tablespoon of butter and 1 tablespoon of olive oil to the skillet, brown chicken pieces (skin side down first), then place in baking pan. Cut onions, carrots, potatoes, and mushrooms (optional) into chunks and brown them in the same skillet. Add flour to skillet with fat stirring until brown (add more oil if needed). Add brandy and flambé. Stir until flame subsides. Add dry white wine or vermouth, tomato paste, thyme, bay leaf, and garlic. Pour mixture over the chicken in baking pan. Add chicken stock if needed for more liquid. Cover tightly. Bake at 350 degrees for 45 minutes. Chicken breasts on bone will take only 30 minutes to bake.

Cranberry-Glazed Sweet Potatoes

yield: 8 servings

Cranberries and sweet potatoes just shout fall! This recipe is adapted from my friend Olga, who uses it in her home cooking classes.

4 pounds sweet potatoes, peeled and cut crosswise in ¼-inch slices

4 tablespoons butter, melted

2 tablespoons bourbon

salt and pepper

¾ cup cranberries

⅓ cup light brown sugar

⅛ teaspoon cayenne pepper

⅛ teaspoon cinnamon

Preheat oven to 350 degrees and butter a large, shallow baking dish. Arrange sweet potatoes in concentric circles, overlapping slightly. Pour ½ cup of water over potatoes. In small bowl, mix melted butter with bourbon. Spoon mixture over sweet potatoes. Season with salt and pepper; cover with foil and bake for about 25 minutes. Baste with liquid in pan and continue cooking until tender and liquid is gone.

Meanwhile, in saucepan, combine cranberries, ⅓ cup of water, and brown sugar and boil over moderately high heat until cranberries start to burst, about 10 minutes. Drain cranberries, reserving the liquid separately (if not much liquid remains, skip draining, and add cranberry sauce in its entirety over potatoes). Stir cayenne and cinnamon into cranberry liquid and spoon it over potatoes. Bake, basting well after 5 minutes, for 20 minutes longer, until potatoes are nicely glazed and most of the liquid has been absorbed. During last 5 minutes of baking, scatter cranberries on top. Serve warm.

Roasted Pork Loin

yield: 6 - 8 servings

You can platter this up with thinner slices and garnish with fresh vegetables such as Brussel sprouts, horsetail carrot (baby carrots with tops), haricot verts, and beets.

1 (5-pound) pork loin

2 pounds frozen chopped spinach, thawed and drained

1 cup toasted pine nuts (optional)

3 cups crumbled feta

2 tablespoons roasted garlic puree

salt and pepper to taste

butcher's twine for trussing

Clean and filet pork loin until it is a thin flat surface (you can ask your local butcher to do this). Spread out on a parchment-lined counter. In a bowl, add spinach, pine nuts, feta, garlic, salt, and pepper and mix well. Spread mixture all over the pork, leaving a 1-inch border on the top and bottom. Once evenly spread, take the bottom of the pork and roll it to the top. Keep it tight but not so tight that the filling falls out from the side. Using twine, tie pork roulade every 2 to 3 inches. Place on a dripping rack on a baking pan or sheet and season with salt and pepper. Bake at 350 degrees for 15-20 minutes or until the meat's temperature reaches 150 degrees. Pull out of oven and let rest for 5 minutes. Cut into 1 ½- to 2-inch slices. Take off twine. Serve warm.

Lobster Mac N' Cheese

yield: 8 - 10 servings

This recipe definitely takes a classic comfort food up a notch! We've served this in individual ramekins for parties or in a casserole for buffets.

16 ounces elbow macaroni

4 cups milk

4 sticks butter

½ cup flour

2 ½ cups parmesan, grated

2 cups sharp white cheddar

16 ounces lobster meat, cooked and diced

salt and pepper

1 tablespoon lobster base (optional)

Preheat oven to 350 degrees. Grease a 9x13 casserole dish with butter. Cook pasta according to directions on package. Drain well. Heat milk in a saucepan. Heat butter until melted and add flour. Whisk for 2 minutes and slowly add to milk, stirring constantly until smooth. Add parmesan and cheddar to sauce. Stir until smooth. Add salt and pepper to taste. Add cooked lobster meat and combine with pasta. Pour into a 13x9 casserole dish.

Topping

2 cups panko breadcrumbs

½ cup parmesan, grated

¼ cup butter, melted

Combine panko, parmesan, and butter. Sprinkle evenly over macaroni and lobster mixture. Bake at 350 degrees for 25-30 minutes or until golden brown.

Pumpkin Roulade

yield: 1 log (12 slices)

Such a beautiful autumn dessert! This roulade may be made ahead and frozen or kept in the fridge for 2-3 days before serving.

1 cup sugar

¾ cup flour

1 teaspoon baking powder

1 teaspoon cinnamon

½ teaspoon ginger

¼ teaspoon cloves

salt, pinch

3 eggs

2/3 cup canned pumpkin

Preheat oven to 350 degrees. Line 10 ½ x 15 ½ jelly roll pan with parchment and spray. In mixing bowl, combine sugar, flour, baking powder, cinnamon, ginger, cloves, and salt. In separate bowl, combine eggs with pumpkin and mix well. Then, add to dry mixture and mix until just combined. Pour in prepared pan, spread evenly, and bake until toothpick comes out clean, about 15 minutes. Lay down kitchen towel, sprinkle powder sugar over towel. While cake is still hot, roll up in the towel and allow to cool. Once cool, fill with filling mixture and cover with filling mixture or dust with powdered sugar.

Filling

8 ounces cream cheese

1 cup powdered sugar

2 tablespoons butter, softened

1 teaspoon vanilla

½ cup walnuts, finely chopped

In a mixer fitted with paddle attachment, cream together cream cheese and butter until smooth. Add vanilla and mix until incorporated. Scrape sides of bowl. Slowly add powdered sugar and continue to mix until incorporated and smooth. Mix in walnuts. Cover until ready to use. If making ahead, keep covered and refrigerate. Before using, take out and let it come to room temperature or mix in mixer again till pliable.

Pumpkin Seed Brittle

yield: 16 servings

This yummy brittle makes a lovely garnish for fall desserts or can stand alone as a candy.

non-stick vegetable oil spray

1 cup sugar

½ cup light corn syrup

3 tablespoons water

1 cup raw pumpkin seeds (pepitas), shelled

2 tablespoons unsalted butter

1 teaspoon kosher salt

¾ teaspoon baking soda

⅛ teaspoon ground cinnamon

¼ teaspoon flaky sea salt

Spray a parchment-lined baking sheet or use Silpat and set aside. In medium saucepan over medium heat, bring sugar, corn syrup, and water to a boil, stirring to dissolve sugar. Fit saucepan with candy thermometer and cook until thermometer registers 290 degrees, 3-4 minutes. Stir in pumpkin seeds, butter, and salt and cook, stirring often, until pale brown and thermometer registers 305 degrees, 3-4 minutes. Stir in baking soda and cinnamon (mixture will bubble vigorously), then immediately pour caramel onto prepared sheet. Using a heatproof spatula, quickly spread out and sprinkle with sea salt; let cool. Break brittle into pieces. Brittle can be made 1 week ahead and stored at room temperature in an airtight container with parchment paper between each layer.

Crème Anglaise

yield: 3 cups

This classic sauce is a complement to so many desserts. It can dress up a basic pound cake topped with fruit or serve as the filling or topping of a dessert roulade.

2 cups half-and-half

½ cup sugar

1 vanilla bean

4 egg yolks

In heavy sauce pot, mix cream and sugar. Split and scrape vanilla bean and add to mix. Lightly beat eggs until smooth. Bring cream mix to a strong boil and temper into yolks. Place in ice bath and stir to chill. Do not stir with whip. Pass through fine strainer.

Moscow Mule Drink

yield: 1 drink

This is traditionally served in a Moscow Mule copper mug. We've had more and more grooms request this as their signature drink at weddings. The copper cups make a wonderful groomsman's gift.

1 ½ ounces vodka

¾ ounces fresh lime juice

3 ounces ginger beer

lime wheel

Fill glass with ice, add all ingredients, and garnish with a lime wheel.

Let Nature Be the Inspiration

Go to your local farmers' markets and load up on baby pumpkins, large pumpkins, gourds, and squash. I love to make seasonal displays on my sideboard. When leaves start to turn, I enjoy picking some branches to add to my design. Fresh fruits such as pears and apples can be added as well. Layering your display is always important to give it more interest. Use rustic pieces like copper, wood, or pottery to add texture to the presentation.

I love Grammercy Tavern in New York, which always has a fantastic seasonal floral display—by the talented Roberta Bendavid—that sets the perfect tone.

tailgate party

In the South, we plan our lives around SEC football. When you're choosing a date for a wedding, a charity fundraiser, or a black tie gala, the football schedule is considered. We take our football seriously, not just because it's fun to watch but because it's fun to watch together. It's a pastime ripe with tradition, something that connects us in a big way, a ritual we welcome year after year, an important part of autumn revelry. Tailgating is an integral part of the football festivities. You'll want to serve a wide variety of food: definitely at least one entrée you can grill fresh, appetizers you can make a few days ahead, some side salads, a dessert, and tasty drinks that look fancy but are actually really easy.

Mini Grilled Spicy Pimento Sandwiches

yield: 2 cups

This pimento cheese is fabulous in the sandwiches and works just as well as a dip for your favorite vegetables or crackers. Adding some sriracha gives it more zip!

Pimento Cheese

1 pound cheddar cheese

3 large roasted peppers, chopped

½ cup mayonnaise

splash Tabasco or Sriracha

In mixing bowl with paddle attachment, combine all ingredients.

Grilled Pimento Sandwiches

yield: 6 tea sandwiches

8 pieces white bread

2 cups pimento cheese

1 stick melted butter

Spread 8 tablespoons of pimento cheese on 4 slices of bread and top with remaining 4 slices. Heat a non-stick skillet to medium-high heat. While pan is coming up to temperature, brush both sides of bread with butter. Once pan is hot, add sandwiches and cook until golden brown on both sides. Remove from pan, cut into 4 triangles, and serve warm.

Beef Brisket Sliders
with Blackberry Onion Jam on Pretzel Bun

yield: 12

Beef Brisket

(see pot roast recipe, page 122)

Blackberry Syrup

2 cups frozen blackberries

½ cup cold water

½ cup brown sugar

2 tablespoons cornstarch slurry (equal parts cold water and cornstarch)

In a saucepot, heat blackberries with water on high heat until mixture comes to a boil. Add sugar. Once dissolved, remove from heat and let cool slightly. Puree berries in blender and strain to remove seeds. Return to saucepot and cook on medium heat. Add slurry mixture until you have a syrup consistency.

Blackberry Onion Jam

1 ounce olive oil

1 large red onion, cut into thin strips, chiffonade

2 tablespoons red wine vinegar

3 ounces blackberry syrup

salt to taste

Sauté onion with oil on medium heat until translucent. Add vinegar and blackberry syrup. Simmer for 2 minutes. If desired, season with salt.

For assembly: Using purchased pretzel rolls or mini Kaiser rolls, add the brisket, top with onion jam and store-bought slaw.

Hot Spinach Dip

yield: 2 quarts

You can make this dip a couple of hours ahead of time, just keep it in a thermos or crockpot so it's warm when you're ready to serve it Add chopped artichoke hearts as a flavorful option.

Roux

2 sticks butter

I cup flour

In small pot over medium heat, melt butter and gradually whisk in flour. Continue to cook on medium heat for 2-3 minutes until mixture starts to boil, while stirring continuously. Remove from heat and set aside.

Dip

I ½ quarts whole milk

I cup roux

I ½ cups parmesan, grated

8 ounces frozen spinach, thawed and drained, excess water squeezed out

pinch of cayenne, or to taste

I teaspoon hot sauce

2 teaspoons roasted garlic powder

salt and white pepper to taste

In medium saucepot, bring milk to a simmer (not boiling). Once milk is steaming and simmering, whisk in the roux, ¼ cup at a time, stirring constantly until consistency is a thick cream sauce. Lower burner to low heat and add parmesan gradually while continuing to whisk. Once cheese is incorporated and melted, add spinach, cayenne, hot sauce, garlic powder, salt and pepper. Serve with tortilla chips.

Truffled Popcorn

yield: 5 cups

To add some extra pop at the party, serve the popcorn in paper cones.

4 tablespoons butter

2 teaspoons truffle oil

1 bag microwave popcorn (or fresh popcorn)

1 cup parmesan

salt to taste

In large bowl, melt butter and add truffle oil. Pop popcorn according to package. Pour popped popcorn into large bowl and toss with butter and truffle oil. Add parmesan and salt. Serve warm at room temperature.

Pigs in a Blanket

yield: 20

Everybody's got their favorite sauce for their "pigs in a blanket." Use your favorite for dipping the sausage! We prefer the rich flavor of whole-grain mustard.

1 pound Conecuh sausage

1 package frozen or refrigerated pie dough

2 eggs

1 tablespoon water

whole-grain mustard

Cut sausage into 2-inch pieces. If using frozen pie dough, thaw it for 15-20 minutes and cut into 1-inch strips. Combine eggs and water in a bowl and whisk briskly. Wrap sausage in the pie dough just until dough overlaps. Cut away excess dough and use the egg wash to close. Bake in 350 degree oven for 15-20 minutes or until golden brown.

White Chili with Chicken

yield: 2 gallons

We've lightened up on traditional chili using chicken and white beans. For football watching, it's really fun to have a chili bar with a variety of toppings: grated cheddar, diced avocado, chopped onions, chopped bacon, and sour cream.

3 tablespoons olive oil

2 large yellow onions, chopped

5 cloves garlic, minced

1 ½ cups chili powder

½ cup ground coriander

2 (12-ounce) cans navy beans, rinsed

4 pounds whole chicken breasts, skinned, boned, and cut into cubes (can be half breast and half thighs)

1 (12-ounce) pale ale beers

10 large tomatoes, diced

4 cups light chicken stock

salt to taste

1 ½ teaspoons cinnamon, ground

Heat half the olive oil in a Dutch oven over high heat. Add onion and garlic and sauté over medium heat. Stir in chili powder, coriander, and cinnamon and cook for 5 minutes more. Remove from heat and set aside. Brown chicken in batches in the remaining 3 tablespoons of oil in a large skillet just until cooked through. Add chicken, beans, tomatoes with the puree, and beer (optional) to the Dutch oven and stir to combine. Simmer over medium heat for 15 minutes. Season with salt to taste. Garnish with sliced scallions, sour cream, grated cheddar cheese, and diced avocados.

Lamb and Black Bean Chili

yield: 1 gallon

This is another variation for your chili party. I've used this same recipe with ground turkey if that's preferred.

6 tablespoons olive oil

2 medium onions, chopped

4 cloves garlic, minced

1 sweet red pepper, finely chopped

1 pound lamb meat, ground

1 (14-ounce) can crushed tomatoes

1 cup tomato sauce

2 tablespoons tomato paste

2 tablespoons masa flour or cornstarch mixed with ½ cup cold water

8 cups chicken stock

2 (15-ounce) cans black beans

2 teaspoons chopped chilies or small can green chilies

2 tablespoons chili powder

1 teaspoon cumin

1 teaspoon coriander

½ teaspoon cayenne

1 teaspoon salt

¼ cup cilantro, chopped (for garnish)

In Dutch oven on medium-high heat, sauté onion, garlic, and red pepper in olive oil, stirring constantly until vegetables are soft. Add ground lamb, and cook until meat is done. Add tomatoes, tomato sauce, tomato paste, flour water mixture, and beer. Stir in black beans and remaining ingredients except for cilantro. Cover and reduce heat and simmer for 20-30 minutes. Top with chopped cilantro. Other optional toppings include grated jack or cheddar cheese, sour cream, chopped onions, and chopped peppers.

New Potato Salad

yield: 6 servings

Warm new potatoes are tossed with shallots and vinaigrette dressing, then cooled and finished with a touch of mayonnaise or sour cream. This is a very flavorful recipe and a different twist on traditional potato salad.

Vinaigrette Dressing

1 ½ tablespoons tarragon vinegar

½ teaspoon Dijon mustard

1 garlic clove, minced

4 ½ tablespoons olive oil

½ teaspoon salt

½ teaspoon pepper

2 shallots (may substitute 4 green onions), minced

In a small bowl, combine vinegar, mustard, garlic, and shallots. Gradually whisk in oil, then add salt and pepper.

Potato Salad

2 ½ pounds new potatoes

2 tablespoons mayonnaise or sour cream

¾ cup celery, diced

½ cup green onions

½ cup fresh dill (or 1 ½ teaspoons dried dillweed), chopped

2 tablespoons fresh parsley, minced

In large pot, cover potatoes with salted water. Cover and boil gently until just tender. Drain and cool slightly. Slice warm potatoes and place in large bowl. Toss with vinaigrette, then let stand 30 minutes. Mix mayonnaise or sour cream, celery, green onions, and herbs into potatoes. Adjust seasonings to taste. Cover and refrigerate. Serve at room temperature. Can be prepared one day ahead.

Dad's Famous BBQ Sauce with Maker's Mark

yield: 8 - 10 servings

This is definitely a family favorite. If it's not hot enough for you, add more cayenne or a little hot sauce.

1 ½ cups apple cider vinegar

1 teaspoon salt

1 pinch black pepper

3 tablespoons brown sugar

2 tablespoons Worcestershire sauce

2 cups ketchup

3 tablespoons mustard

2 tablespoon lemon juice

3 bay leaves

¼ teaspoon cayenne

3 cups reduced to 1 cup Maker's Mark

Mix vinegar, salt, black pepper Worcestershire, sugar, ketchup, and mustard. Slowly cook on low. Add lemon juice, bay leaves, and cayenne. Cook for at least 30 minutes. Add reduced Maker's Mark.

Tennessee Honey Lemonade

yield: 1 serving

This is delicious and can be made up in gallon jugs for tailgating. Add ice and serve. We've also use Cathead Honeysuckle Vodka from Mississippi instead of Bourbon.

Make Caramelized Lemonade (page 87).

In a glass, add 2 ounces of Jack Daniels Tennessee Honey whiskey, or equal whisky. Pour lemonade over whiskey and stir. Serve over ice.

Tailgating 101

Even if you don't have a truck with an actual tailgate, you can set up your tailgating party with whatever you've got. We've used a 6-foot or 8-foot buffet table and folded up one end and had it come out from the trunk of an SUV or car. You need to level the other end with the legs extended with wooden crates or blocks to have a flat table. Dress with your team colors and spread out your buffet—think chili, warm dips, savory chips, and comfort food of all sorts. Make your bloody mary's memorable by garnishing with a mini slider on a pick. Designing team cake pops and lining them up on a green styro playing field makes a fun display. Goal posts are fun and easy to make with pipe cleaners.

holiday tables

Even non-cooks entertain during the holidays. You just can't escape it, though who would want to! Every family has a few special once-a-year dishes that everybody looks forward to. You can try making them an extra time, say for Christmas in July, but it's just not the same. Pair these special family favorites with some of our tried-and-true recipes and you're sure to make a big splash at your holiday gatherings. In your planning, keep the reason for the season foremost in mind. When you put the people first and design the meal and festivities accordingly, the conversation will flow freely, everyone will love the food, and you'll be making more special memories than you can count.

Holiday Dinner in a Glass

yield: as desired

Try a decorative and non-traditional way to serve your holiday meals! Layering Thanksgiving dinner in a martini glass makes for a beautiful presentation.

mashed potatoes

dressing/stuffing

sliced baked turkey

gravy

cranberry compote

Layer ingredients in a martini glass, starting with mashed potatoes on the bottom.

Duck Confit w/ Mango Salsa on Icebox Crackers Bun

yield: 20 pieces

This is a labor of love but so good.

Parmesan Rosemary Icebox Crackers

1 ½ cups flour

2 teaspoons salt

pinch white pepper

4 teaspoons rosemary, chopped

2 ounces butter

2 cups parmesan

⅓ cup sour cream

In food processor, add flour, salt, pepper, and rosemary and pulse to combine. Add butter and pulse until mixture resembles coarse meal. Add parmesan and pulse until combined. Add 1 tablespoon of sour cream at a time, pulsing each time to combine. Process until dough comes together and is well combined. Transfer dough to a clean work surface and shape into a 2-inch-wide log. Wrap log with plastic wrap and refrigerate for at least 24 hours.

Heat oven to 325 degrees. Slice well-chilled log into ¼-inch-thick slices. Bake immediately until crackers are golden brown and firm in the center, 25-30 minutes. Transfer to a rack to cool.

Duck Confit

4 duck leg portions, thighs attached, excess fat trimmed and reserved (about 2 pounds)

I tablespoon plus 1/8 teaspoon kosher salt

1/2 teaspoon freshly ground black pepper

10 garlic cloves

4 bay leaves

4 sprigs fresh thyme

I 1/2 teaspoons black peppercorns

1/2 teaspoon table salt

4 cups olive oil

6-8 cups duck fat, purchased at specialty store

2 tablespoons shallots, chopped

I tablespoon parsley, chopped

mango salsa

Lay the leg portions on a platter, skin side down. Marinate the duck legs with I tablespoon kosher salt and 1/2 teaspoon black pepper, with garlic, thyme, and one bay leaf on each leg. Sprinkle with remaining 1/8 teaspoon kosher salt. Cover and refrigerate for 12 hours.

Preheat the oven to 200 degrees. Remove duck from refrigerator. Remove garlic, bay leaves, thyme, and duck fat and reserve. Rinse duck with cool water, rubbing off some of the salt and pepper. Pat dry with paper towels. Put reserved garlic, bay leaves, thyme, and duck fat in bottom of an enameled cast-iron pot. Sprinkle evenly with the peppercorns and salt. Lay duck on top, skin side

down, and add olive oil. Cover and bake for 6-8 hours, or until meat pulls away from the bone. Remove duck from the fat. Strain fat and reserve. Pick the meat from the bones and place it in a bowl. Mix duck with chopped shallots and parsley. Assembly: Add I teaspoon of duck mixture on icebox crackers and garnish with mango salsa.

Mango Salsa

2 cups mangoes, diced

I tablespoon fresh garlic, minced

3 tablespoons fresh cilantro, chopped

3 tablespoons lime juice

1/2 cup red bell pepper, diced

1/4 cup red onion, diced

3 tablespoons olive oil

salt to taste

jalapeno, seeded and minced, to taste

Mix all ingredients together and refrigerate.

Sugared Cranberries on Brie and Cracker

yield: 16 servings

Such a simple easy way to bring in the season! I love to line a tray with cranberries to provide a holiday background to any hors d'oeuvre.

2 cups fresh cranberries

1 cup maple syrup

1 cup granulated sugar

16 crackers

8 ounces Brie

cranberry chutney or relish

fresh mint for garnish

½ cup honey

2 star anise

Rinse cranberries and place in medium bowl. Heat syrup, honey, and anise in a small saucepan just until warm. Take out star anise. Pour over cranberries when syrup is warm, not hot! Cranberries may pop if syrup is too hot. In medium bowl, pour warm syrup over washed cranberries, cover, and let steep overnight. Drain cranberries in colander. Place sugar in large bowl or baking dish. Add cranberries in two batches and roll around until lightly coated in sugar. Place on baking sheet until dry, about an hour.

Assemble crackers with one slice of brie, a light layer of cranberry chutney, and 4 to 5 candied cranberries. Garnish with fresh mint.

Peppermint Meringue Twist

yield: 32 (2-inch) meringues

Such a quick and easy sweet that melts in your mouth. The chocolate ganache in the center puts it over the top!

3 egg whites

¾ cup sugar

⅛ teaspoon peppermint oil

red gel food coloring as needed for bag

peppermint, chopped for garnish

Heat egg whites and sugar over water bath until it reaches 110 degrees, or hot to touch. Whip until stiff peaks form and beat in peppermint oil. Carefully paint two lines along the seams of the piping bag with the food coloring halfway up the bag, using a thin paint brush.

Fit bag with ¼-inch round tip or star tip. Fill with meringue, trying not to smear the gel. Line cookie pan with parchment paper, spraying the pan with pan spray. Pipe a full base in small circles, starting from the center and working out to make a 2-inch base. Pipe up the outsides of the base until it forms ¾- to 1-inch-tall cups. Bake in 200-degree oven for 20-30 minutes or until it easily comes off the parchment paper. Let cool completely and wrap tightly while still on the cookie sheet, or store in airtight container. Fill with a chocolate ganache or a buttercream frosting of choice and add garnish.

Chocolate Ganache

12 ounces semi-sweet chocolate chips

1 ½ cups heavy cream

1 tablespoon butter

1 tablespoon honey

Bring cream, butter, and honey to a boil. In mixing bowl, pour mixture over chocolate chips and wisk until smooth. Cool until mixture starts to set and then whip in stand mixer.

Pot de Crème

yield: 4 servings

My absolute favorite dessert, this is so decadent! I love to serve it in a demitasse cup. Remember, the better the chocolate, the better the custard. I prefer Valrhona dark.

1 cup half-and-half

8 ounces semi-sweet chocolate

2 teaspoons sugar

3 egg yolks

½ teaspoon vanilla

In a pot bring half-and-half, chocolate, and sugar to boil. Slowly pour chocolate mixture into egg yolks while whisking. Return mixture to pot and cook over a low heat for 2 minutes. Remove from heat and stir in vanilla. Pour through fine mesh strainer and fill cups. Refrigerate overnight to set.

Mom's Jelly Roll

yield: 1 roll or 13 slices

Mom's special homemade sponge cake filled with raspberry jam is a wonderful recipe for breakfast or brunch. Dust it with powdered sugar just before serving.

3 eggs, separated

1 ½ cups flour

1 ½ tablespoons baking powder

1 ¼ cups sugar

¾ cup milk

1 teaspoon vanilla

1 ½ tablespoons shortening

2 tablespoons powdered sugar

1 jar jelly (your favorite)

Preheat oven to 350 degrees. Beat egg whites to stiff peaks in an electric mixer and set aside. Scald milk over medium high heat. Whisk sugar into the egg yolks then slowly add the hot milk. Add the shortening then stir in flour and baking powder. Fold in the whipped egg whites and vanilla. Spread evenly in a greased jelly roll pan and bake at 350 for 20 minutes. Let cool slightly. Lay out a clean kitchen towel on the counter and sprinkle with powdered sugar. Turn out the cake onto the towel and cover with an even layer of jelly. Using the towel to help, roll up the cake and dust with powdered sugar.

Holiday Caramel Sticks

yield: 30 pieces

Holidays brings back memories of all the wonderful aromas of homemade sweets—the ones we grew up enjoying.

1 stick of butter

2 cups brown sugar

2 cups flour

2 cups pecans

2 eggs

2/3 cup dried cherries

2/3 cup dried cranberries

2 teaspoons baking powder

1 teaspoon salt

1 teaspoon vanilla

Melt butter in a small pot over medium high heat. Stir in sugar and continue to cook for 2 minutes to caramelize slightly. Combine flour, pecans, dried fruits, baking powder, and salt in mixing bowl. Stir butter mixture into flour until combined. Stir in the eggs and vanilla. Pour into a greased 13x9 baking dish and bake at 350 for 25-30 minutes or until set. Cool on baking rack then cut into 2 × 2 pieces and dust with powder sugar and your favorite holiday sprinkles.

A. B.'s Pound Cake

yield: 1 loaf pan or 1 bundt pan

My dad's "no-fail" pound cake is perfect every time! Start with a cold oven and cook for 1 hour and 15 minutes. It's a great base for berries and sauce or just serve it toasted with butter for breakfast.

2 sticks of butter (½ pound), softened

3 cups flour

3 cups sugar

1 cup milk

5 eggs

½ teaspoon vanilla

½ teaspoon baking powder

Cream butter and sugar in electric mixer. Add eggs one at a time. Sift baking powder with flour. Add flour and then milk alternately a little at a time until all incorporated. Mix in vanilla until very smooth and velvety. Pour into a greased, paper-lined loaf pan. Put in a cold oven. Bake at 350 for about 1 hour and 15 minutes. Bake until inserted toothpick comes out clean.

Eggnog Cheesecake

yield: 9-inch cheesecake

Simply decadent and delicious! Thanks to Jeff for this divine holiday dessert. It truly melts in your mouth.

Crust

2 cups graham cracker crumbs

3 ounces butter, melted

¼ cup brown sugar

In a bowl, mix ingredients. Press into sprayed pie pan. Bake at 325 degrees for 8-12 minutes, or until crust is golden brown.

Filling

2 pounds cream cheese

1 cup sugar

2 tablespoons flour

2 teaspoons nutmeg

½ teaspoon cinnamon

1 teaspoon vanilla

3 tablespoons rum (bourbon or brandy)

1 cup heavy cream

2 eggs

4 egg yolks

Preheat oven to 325 degrees. In mixer, cream together cream cheese and sugar until smooth. Add flour, nutmeg, cinnamon, vanilla, and rum. Slowly stir in heavy cream, then eggs and egg yolks one at a time. Pour over crust and bake for 30-45 minutes.

Holiday Milk Punch

yield: 1 drink

So yummy and definitely rings in the season!

1 ½ ounces good bourbon or brandy

2 ounces half-and-half

1 teaspoon superfine sugar

drop of vanilla extract

ice cubes

freshly grated nutmeg

Combine bourbon, half-and-half, sugar, and vanilla in a cocktail shaker with ice. Shake thoroughly until mixture is cold and frothy. Strain into a highball glass filled with ice. Top with a grating of nutmeg.

Fruit-infused Cocktails

Infused vodkas make a festive and colorful display on the bar. Guests can choose their favorite flavor and then you can shake it in an ice-filled martini shaker, strain, and serve.

a fifth Smirnoff vanilla-flavored vodka

1 cup sugar

1 cup water

2 cups of fresh pineapple, diced

Make a simple syrup by boiling water and sugar. Take a fifth of vanilla-flavored vodka and pour in a sterilized jar. Add 2 cups diced fresh pineapple, and simple syrup.

Holiday Decorating 101

Break out the festive chargers and color-coordinated linens. Go crazy with sprigs of holiday greenery on the platters, tables, and everywhere else you can think of—it's an easy touch that makes a huge impact in setting the holiday tone. Try bright red apples paired with a turquoise linen. We love to do tons of cranberries. Think sprinkled around trays, topping appetizers, in clear vessels of every shape and size, floating in bowls, in trays of candles. And of course boiled, sweetened, and served with a very large spoon. Cranberries and these other symbols of holiday cheer make you happy and that's what the season is all about.

acknowledgements

This book would not have been possible without the creativity, hard work and dedication of the Culinary Team of Kathy G & Company, especially Chef Angie Griffin Klose and Andy Hopper, AIFD with KG Designs.

Special thanks to Arden Photography, Arden Ward Upton and Moesia Davis, for going beyond the call of duty and friendship.

Thanks to Michelle Van Every, David Haugen and Christopher Confero of Alabama Weddings Magazine, Bromberg's Fine Jewelry and Tabletop, the Historic Donnelly House, the Nest in Avondale.

Thanks to my dear friend, Olga Lembesis for her friendship and guidance through the years.

And lastly, thank you to the many photographers, listed below, that I have had the pleasure of working with over the years. and whose work can be enjoyed in this book. Your ability to capture our food and event designs in the precious few moments they are undisturbed and pristine, have made this book possible, but more important...*Fabulous!*.

photography credits

Arden Photography

A Bryan Photo

Alisha Crossley Photography

Angela Karen Photography

Barry Atmark Photography

Beau Gustafson –
   Big Swede Photography

Beth Hontzas Photography

Brad Roller Photography

Breanna Fogg Photography

Chanterelle Photography

Daniel Taylor Photography

Fotowerks

Frank Carnaggio Photography

Gretchen B Photography

Heather Durham Photography

J Messer Photography

Jeanne Clayton

Jerrod Brown Studios

Jonathon Davis Phoyography

J Woodbery Photography

Lacy Robinson Photography

Marsha Perry Photography

Matt Matthews Photography

Moesia Davis Photography

Photography by Shea

Rob Ingram Photography

Studio G

index

index